12

Habits of
Successful SEOs

Staying Effective in an AI-Driven Search Landscape

Ash Nallawalla

12 Habits of Successful SEOs / Ash Nallawalla.

Subjects:

1. Search engine optimization.
2. Digital marketing—Professional practice.
3. Online visibility management.
4. Artificial intelligence—Information retrieval.
5. Website performance and governance.

Classification: HF5548.8; 658.8—dc23

BUS043000 — Business & Economics / Marketing / Digital

COM060140 — Computers / Web / Search Engines Optimization

Disclaimer: All information has been presented in good faith, using information believed to be accurate at the time of publication. Use the information at your own risk. Errors and omissions are excepted.

First Edition

ISBN: 978-1-7644704-2-1

PREFACE

Two decades in SEO teach you that the work never stands still. The last five years have made that clearer than ever. The foundational signals—links, relevance, technical optimization—still matter, but they now operate inside a far more complex ecosystem shaped by machine learning, entity understanding, and AI-mediated retrieval. Search used to feel like a system of rules you could master. Today, it behaves more like a living environment, constantly reinterpreting information across new interfaces.

The shift became impossible to ignore the first time I saw a client hold strong organic rankings but missing from AI-generated summaries. High visibility in traditional search, but zero presence on new surfaces. That disconnect revealed something essential: ranking well and being retrieved well are no longer the same challenge.

This evolution has changed what it means to be an effective SEO professional. The practitioners who consistently succeed aren't the ones who memorize the most ranking factors or collect the most tools. They're the ones who've developed durable professional habits.

Early in an SEO career, it's easy to chase whatever tactic is working this month. Every algorithm update feels like a reset. Every industry shift feels like a threat. That reactive posture creates a career defined by scrambling.

12 Habits of Successful SEOs

The people who endure work differently. They build intuition through experience. They test new ideas on their own properties before touching production. They operate on habits that keep them effective regardless of changes.

This book is about those habits.

THE TWELVE HABITS

This book covers 12 habits that set consistently effective SEO practitioners apart from those who feel perpetually behind. These habits aren't personality traits. They're learnable, repeatable skills you can begin applying immediately.

The habits are:

Foundation Habits — Building your baseline capabilities

- Continuous Learning
- Data-Driven Decision-Making
- Technical Precision

Execution Habits — Delivering effective work

- Content with Purpose
- Relentless User Focus
- Strategic Link Building

System Habits — Operating within organizations

- Adaptability to Change
- Collaboration Without Friction
- Process Discipline

Strategic Habits — Thinking beyond the immediate

- Strategic Patience
- Ethical Integrity
- Visionary Thinking

These habits reinforce one another. Technical precision strengthens collaboration. User focus improves content. Continuous learning sharpens data interpretation. Together, they form a complete professional practice.

INDUSTRY VOICES

I want to thank the 31 industry professionals who contributed their perspectives on the 12 habits in the appendices.

WHO THIS BOOK SERVES

This book is for SEO operators—the people who do the actual work of audits, content optimization, technical implementation, link development, and cross-functional collaboration.

You might be agency-side, managing 8-15 clients with limited hours per account, juggling industries, platforms, and personalities, often without direct access to developers. You might be in-house at a single brand, where you see the same site every day and navigate internal politics, competing priorities, and the challenge of proving SEO value. You might manage multiple properties with different CMSs, stakeholders, and release cycles. Or you might be a freelancer or consultant, serving as a strategist, implementer, and business owner all at once.

The habits apply across all of these environments. What "continuous learning" looks like for an agency SEO differs from what it looks like for someone managing a massive e-commerce platform—but the underlying discipline is the same.

HOW TO USE THIS BOOK

Each chapter stands alone. You can read straight through or jump to the habits you need most. Each chapter includes why the habit matters, how it shows up in daily work, common failure patterns, and practical ways to develop it.

Examples throughout this book have been altered, time-shifted, or blended to protect **confidentiality**. Some stories are composites. All reflect real patterns and genuine lessons.

WHAT COMES NEXT

These twelve habits mark the difference between SEO as a list of tasks and SEO as a craft. You already have the technical knowledge. What you're building now is the professional maturity that determines how far that knowledge takes you.

These habits won't make you perfect. They'll make you resilient, effective, and able to thrive as search continues to evolve. Let's begin.

HABIT 1: CONTINUOUS LEARNING

THE MOMENT THE GROUND SHIFTED

When I first got into SEO, I thought I had it mostly figured out. I could audit a site, tidy up content, chase links from high-authority pages, and explain everything in a way that made stakeholders nod along. It felt like a system I understood.

Then Google changed the rules—not with the language we use today, like "entities," but with a shift in how it understood relationships between concepts. We didn't have the vocabulary for it back then, but we definitely felt the impact. Rankings slipped in ways that didn't match the old playbook. Fixes that used to work suddenly felt weak. Once-easy conversations became awkward because the explanations no longer fit what we were seeing.

So I went back to school, in a sense. I spent hours reading research papers instead of blog posts, running experiments on sites where breaking things didn't matter, and comparing notes with people who were already adapting. I had a network of small affiliate sites at the time—simple script-based catalogs that ranked well until the Florida update wiped them out. That gave me a low-stakes sandbox to rebuild, test, and watch how Google reacted when failure was cheap.

It was exhausting, but it taught me something I should've realized earlier: in SEO, learning isn't something you finish. It's the job. The people who stay effective aren't the ones who learned SEO once—they're the ones who are still learning this week.

To this day, I have a site documenting a European river cruise my wife and I took over ten years ago. It has a review of the cruise product and a daily blog of what we saw, with photos and videos. It is monetized with Google AdSense, so my hosting costs are covered.

HOW THE PLATEAU HAPPENS QUIETLY

Most SEOs don't stop learning on purpose. It just happens.

You get good at something. People trust you. Your methods keep working. And slowly, without noticing, curiosity gives way to busyness. You stay "up to date" enough to sound current, but you're not really challenging your own thinking anymore.

The slide is subtle. You don't suddenly become outdated. You start noticing that conversations move ahead without you. Newer colleagues reference things you haven't explored yet. Your explanations get longer because you're compensating for gaps you didn't realize were forming.

The industry produces a firehose of content—webinars, podcasts, blog posts—and consuming it all **feels** like learning. But unless it changes how you work, it's just noise.

Real learning is uncomfortable. It means testing ideas, breaking assumptions, and admitting when the evidence contradicts what you believed. Some things you can test on your own sites. Others need staging environments, synthetic data, or collaboration with people who can properly isolate variables.

LEARNING WHEN TIME IS SCARCE

Working in SEO rarely gives you long, peaceful blocks of time to study. Agencies juggle clients. In-house teams fight for engineering resources. Everyone is busy.

What actually works is small, protected pockets of attention. For me, it became a short block at the start of the week that I blocked in my calendar. The length didn't matter. The consistency did.

Those little sessions became a place to poke at one new idea, follow one question far enough to matter, or reflect on something that didn't behave the way I expected.

It's not glamorous, but it's sustainable. And sustainable learning is the only kind that sticks.

HOW LEARNING LOOKS DIFFERENT DEPENDING ON WHERE YOU WORK

Where you work shapes how you learn.

Agency life forces breadth. You bounce between industries, platforms, and constraints so quickly that patterns start to emerge. The risk is that you never go deep enough unless you deliberately slow down. Besides, you cannot take risks with client websites.

In-house life is the opposite. You learn one site inside out. You know every quirk, every template, every compromise. The danger is tunnel vision—you start thinking your company's way is **the** way.

Multi-site or multinational roles add another twist. You see the same issue appear across different properties with slight variations. If you document those patterns instead of solving them in isolation, your learning accelerates fast.

In every environment, continuous learning is really about spotting your blind spots and compensating for them.

HAVING A PLACE WHERE FAILURE IS CHEAP

Some of the best SEO lessons come from breaking things on purpose.

A small, low-stakes site gives you freedom. You can test URL structures, internal linking ideas, schema variations, and content formats—all without approvals, politics, or fear. You get to watch how Google reacts in a clean environment.

Small sites won't teach you everything. They won't show you how crawl budget behaves on a million-URL enterprise site. But they **will** teach you how indexing shifts, how structure influences visibility, and how content behaves when you change the rules.

The real value isn't the results—it's the confidence that testing brings. When you've seen a pattern repeat across controlled tests, you're less reliant on opinions when recommending changes to your work or client sites.

SEPARATING SIGNAL FROM INDUSTRY NOISE

The SEO industry produces a ridiculous volume of commentary. Some of it is brilliant. A lot of it is confident nonsense. Try to identify the names that appear repeatedly in search industry publications and conference speaker lists. Follow them.

Learning slows when you chase every shiny idea. Implementing advice that sounds good but doesn't hold up in practice wastes time and erodes trust.

You develop instincts. Claims backed by clear reasoning or patterns you've seen across multiple contexts feel different from isolated anecdotes. And context matters— what works for a small affiliate site won't necessarily work for a multinational brand.

Part of continuous learning is learning what (or whom) to ignore.

THE LESSONS HIDDEN IN MISINTERPRETATION

Some of the most valuable lessons come from mistakes that look like insights.

I once spent far too long investigating what appeared to be a ranking collapse for a key term. Average position had dropped, so I went into full diagnostic mode—content tweaks, internal links, the whole lot. Nothing moved.

Eventually, I realized the average was hiding multiple pages ranking for that keyword at different depths. The main "money" page was fine. The secondary pages were dragging down the average rank. There was no collapse—just a misleading metric.

That experience changed how I read data. Metrics don't explain themselves. You have to understand how they're constructed before you can trust what they're telling you.

LEARNING FROM WHAT FAILS

Not every experiment works. In fact, most don't.

Schema added where it didn't reflect reality. Internal links added without a strategy. Content length increased without adding value. All of these sounded reasonable until tested. Each one taught a boundary, not a tactic.

Documenting failures matters. Memory is unreliable. Notes prevent you from repeating the same dead ends and sharpen your judgment.

WHEN LEARNING CHANGES THE DIRECTION OF WORK

Continuous learning isn't just about avoiding mistakes. Sometimes it opens doors.

I worked with a financial-services client whose growth had stalled. The breakthrough didn't come from more content or more links. It came from noticing how emerging AI-driven systems were evaluating credibility.

The team had strong credentials, but none of them was visible to systems assessing trust. We ran a small, controlled test to surface that expertise more clearly. The results weren't magical, but they were strong enough to shift our strategy.

That insight didn't come from SEO tools. It came from curiosity outside the immediate task list.

BUILDING THIS HABIT

If you want to make continuous learning stick, here's what tends to work:

Protect a recurring time block. Thirty minutes weekly beats sporadic deep dives. Monday mornings work for many people, before urgency takes over. Use it to explore one new idea, follow one question, or reflect on something that surprised you.

Create a low-stakes testing ground. A side project, a personal site, or access to a staging environment gives you space to break things without consequences. Test one structural change, one schema variation, and one content approach. Watch what happens without the pressure of performance.

Document what you learn. Keep a running note of experiments, failures, and patterns you're starting to see. It doesn't need to be formal. Bullet points work. The act of writing forces lucidity and builds a reference you can return to.

Choose signal over noise. Follow 3-5 sources you trust instead of trying to consume everything. Look for people who show their work, share data, and admit when they're wrong. Unsubscribe from the rest.

Separate learning time from doing time. When you're learning, you're reading, testing, and reflecting. When you're doing, you're executing. Mixing them creates the illusion of productivity without the learning.

Your approach will depend on your constraints. If you're agency-side with limited hours, your learning might focus on pattern recognition across clients. If you're in-house, you might go deeper on your specific platform or industry. If you manage multiple sites, you might focus on documenting how the same issue manifests differently across properties.

The framework is loose on purpose. The discipline is what matters—showing up consistently, staying curious, and treating learning like part of the job instead of something you'll "get to later."

Continuous learning creates the foundation for everything else. Without it, your other habits calcify. Your data interpretation becomes stale. Your technical skills lag. Your content strategies stop evolving. Your ability to adapt weakens.

But when you keep learning, something shifts. You start seeing problems earlier. You recognize patterns faster. You propose solutions grounded in recent evidence, not old assumptions. That credibility opens doors—to better projects, stronger relationships, and work that stays interesting.

The next habit builds on this foundation. Once you've developed the discipline to keep learning, you need a way to turn what you've learned into decisions you can defend. That's where data-driven decision-making comes in—and where many SEOs stumble, even when they have all the information they need.

HABIT 2: DATA-DRIVEN DECISION-MAKING

THE DAY I STOPPED TRUSTING MY GUT

Early-career confidence is a strange thing. You get a few wins, start spotting patterns, and suddenly your brain decides you've developed "instinct." Then you make one expensive mistake and realize you were mostly recognizing your own habits, not the truth.

I once told a client their content "felt thin." I didn't run a proper diagnosis. I didn't challenge my assumptions. I just recommended a full overhaul.

Three months of writer time later, traffic hadn't moved.

When we finally looked properly, the content wasn't the problem at all. Users were landing on pages and getting stuck. Internal linking was a mess. The site had little islands of content with no bridges between them. People would arrive, read one page, and leave because there was no obvious next step.

I'd told the team to rebuild the house when the real issue was that the hallway signs were missing.

That was the moment I stopped treating intuition as a strategy. Working with evidence doesn't guarantee you'll be right—but working with gut feel guarantees you'll be wrong with confidence.

WHY SEOS STRUGGLE WITH DATA EVEN WHEN IT'S RIGHT THERE

Most SEOs don't suffer from a lack of data. They lack time, patience, and a repeatable way to interpret what they're seeing when something starts moving.

The pattern is familiar:

- Traffic drops
- Panic kicks in
- Someone glances at Analytics and sees the dip
- The team starts "fixing" things immediately— rewriting content, changing titles, adding links
- Traffic either recovers on its own or doesn't
- Nobody knows what actually happened

Then the next dip triggers the same scramble.

A traffic drop is emotionally loud. Diagnosis is emotionally quiet. The habit is learning to sit in that quiet long enough to see what's real.

You don't need to become a statistician. You need to stop treating symptoms before you understand the cause.

THE MONDAY ROUTINE THAT SAVED ME FROM GUESSING

I used to think "data-driven" meant building elaborate dashboards. I learned that one consistent weekly rhythm beats five clever reports.

A Short Weekly Check That Catches Problems Early

If you manage multiple clients, you can't deep-dive into each client every week. If you're in-house, you can stare at dashboards all day and still miss the one change that matters.

The solution is a quick scan designed to surface anomalies without turning your week into analytics archaeology.

On Monday mornings, I do a simple review with one goal: spot what looks unusual and isolate what changed first.

I look for:

- Big week-over-week traffic shifts
- Meaningful movement on high-value queries
- Sudden CTR changes
- New Search Console error patterns
- Noticeable performance drops in field data

The key is what happens next: **I don't react immediately.**

I write down what moved and when it started. That tiny pause prevents the classic SEO mistake—fixing the wrong thing quickly.

Turning a Metric Into a Working Theory

Once I've picked the biggest anomaly, I work backward from timing.

I ask three sets of questions:

What changed around the start date? Deployments, content releases, campaigns, migrations.

Where is the change concentrated? Section, device, geography, query type.

What shape does the change have? A cliff, a slope, volatility, isolated URLs, whole templates.

Only then do I write a one-sentence hypothesis. If I can't summarize it in one sentence, I don't understand it yet.

A small habit that helps: write down what you expect to see if your hypothesis is correct. It forces you out of storytelling mode and into test mode.

THE DATA SOURCES THAT MAKE YOU BETTER—AND THE WAYS THEY MISLEAD YOU

Every data source is useful. Every data source can trick you.

Analytics Shows Behavior After Arrival

Analytics tells you what people did once they landed. It doesn't tell you what they wanted, what they searched for, or what your snippet promised them.

Bounce rate is the classic trap. A high bounce rate might mean the page failed—or it might mean the page answered the question instantly. You only know by looking at the time on the page, conversions, and the page's purpose.

Search Console Shows Google's View—Not the Whole Market

Search Console is one of the best windows into how Google treats your site. It's also a great way to confuse yourself if you trust the averages.

I once saw the average position drop for an important query and assumed we were losing. We rewrote and strengthened the page. Nothing changed.

When we drilled down, the "drop" turned out to be just an averaging artifact. Multiple pages were appearing for the same query. One was doing great. Several irrelevant ones were dragging the average down.

That experience taught me: don't trust any aggregate view until you know which URLs are actually driving the metric.

Log Files Tell You What Googlebot Actually Did

Log files are brutally honest. They show what Googlebot crawled, how often, and what it ignored. They don't tell you why, but the patterns usually point you in the right direction.

If you have access (or are not practical in large, busy sites), logs can settle debates instantly. If you don't, you compensate by reading Search Console patterns more carefully and isolating changes to templates, internal links, and index coverage.

AI Retrieval Signals Are a New Kind of Visibility Data

AI surfaces behave differently from rankings. They can cite you even if you're not winning a traditional result—and they can ignore you even when you rank well.

When I check AI summaries, I'm looking for mismatches. If a page ranks well but never appears in AI outputs, it often has issues with coherence or structure. If a competitor is consistently cited, they often have cleaner definitions, tighter entity references, or more extractable statements.

It's messy data, but it's still useful as an early signal.

HOW I STOPPED JUMPING STRAIGHT TO SOLUTIONS

One of the fastest ways to waste time and money in SEO is to diagnose with the conclusion already in mind.

Traffic drops, and the instinctive reaction is, "We need more content. We need more links." Sometimes that's true—but those are expensive levers. When they're wrong, they're wrong in a very slow, very costly way.

The habit that improved my accuracy the most was separating the moment of noticing from the moment of prescribing.

When I see a drop, I want to know:

- What moved
- When it moved
- Where it moved
- What changed around that time

Only then do I decide what to test first. And the first test is almost always smaller than people expect—a segmentation check, an index-coverage review, a deployment correlation, or a device split that reveals where the issue actually lives.

WORKING WITH INCOMPLETE DATA WITHOUT MAKING THINGS UP

You will never have perfect information. Google hides queries. Analytics samples. Users behave unpredictably. AI systems don't explain their retrieval logic. Large sites generate so much noise that real signals can look like random fluctuations.

The practical question is always the same: **Given what I can see, what's the most likely explanation—and what evidence would confirm it?**

Agency Work Forces Fast Pattern Recognition

When you only have a few hours per client each month, you learn to start where reality most often lives. If a traffic drop lines up with a deployment, technical breakage is a sensible first hypothesis. That pattern repeats often enough to be a reliable starting point.

The risk is assuming every client fits the pattern. The habit is verifying quickly before recommending anything expensive.

In-House Work Creates the Opposite Risk

In-house, you can drown in data. When you see every wobble, every daily fluctuation starts to feel like a crisis.

The most practical improvement I've seen in-house teams make is switching to week-over-week and month-over-month review by default. It reduces false alarms and forces attention onto trends that actually persist.

Once you know what "normal" looks like for your site, you stop treating every twitch as a problem.

THE PATTERNS YOU LEARN TO RESPECT—AND THE ONES THAT FOOL YOU

After enough time in SEO, you start recognizing familiar shapes:

- The Friday-deployment drop
- The slow multi-week erosion that hints at competition or SERP shifts
- The seasonal dip that looks scary until you compare year-over-year
- Index-coverage churn that looks dramatic but stabilizes on its own
- Core Web Vitals swings that are measurement noise, not user experience

Pattern recognition is useful—until it isn't. It can make you stop looking closely at the unusual case. The habit is to hold patterns lightly and check them against evidence.

CASE STUDY—THE CONVERSION DROP THAT WASN'T AN SEO ISSUE

An e-commerce client selling home-organization products called in a panic. Organic traffic looked fine, but organic revenue was down 30% month-over-month. They wanted an SEO fix.

The Diagnostic Path

First check: Traffic volume and rankings. Both stable.

Second check: CTR from search. Normal range.

Third check: Behavior on site. Time on site and bounce rate weren't flashing red. Users were reaching product pages and adding to cart at the usual rate.

The break: Conversions were failing at the final step—checkout.

The question: What changed three weeks ago?

Once we treated it as a conversion issue rather than an SEO issue, the answer appeared quickly. They'd introduced a new payment processor. It was failing intermittently on certain Android devices. Users would try to check out, hit an error, and abandon.

The dev team fixed it within a week. Conversions returned.

What This Taught

If I'd followed my instincts, I would've started with rankings, titles, content, and technical checks. Instead, I walked the funnel. Data-driven SEO isn't just about fixing

SEO problems. It's about preventing months of "optimization" when the real failure is downstream.

THE DATA MISTAKES THAT COST YOU TIME AND CREDIBILITY

Most data mistakes don't look like mistakes in the moment.

Correlation confusion: You publish content and traffic grows, so you assume the content caused the growth. Sometimes it did. Sometimes a competitor dropped. Sometimes demand rose. Sometimes an algorithm shift helped you. The habit is looking for mechanisms, not coincidences.

Short-term volatility: Rankings and traffic move constantly. Daily change is rarely decision-making data. Calm comes from choosing timeframes that match how search systems behave.

Aggregate metrics: Averages hide the distribution. Until you see which pages and segments are driving a number, you don't know what's happening.

External factors: Competitors, seasonality, and updates shape your performance whether you acknowledge them or not. Keeping a simple timeline of changes helps you interpret outcomes honestly.

BUILDING THIS HABIT

If you want to make data-driven decision-making stick, here's what tends to work:

Establish a weekly check-in routine. Pick one consistent time—Monday mornings work well—and scan for anomalies. Look for big shifts, not daily noise. Write down what moved and when. Don't react yet.

Write your hypothesis before you investigate. When something looks wrong, write one sentence describing what you think happened. Then write what you'd expect to see if you're right. This forces precision before action.

Segment before you conclude. Don't trust aggregates. Break changes down by device, geography, template, section, or query type. The pattern often lives in a single segment, not across the entire site.

Keep a decision log. Track what you diagnosed, what you recommended, and what happened. Review it quarterly. You'll start seeing your own blind spots and building better judgment.

Build investigation sequences. Create a mental checklist for common scenarios: traffic drops, ranking changes, conversion shifts. Start with the most common causes, then work outward. This prevents random guessing under pressure.

Your approach will vary. If you're agency-side, you might create lightweight templates for each client to spot issues quickly. If you're in-house, you might invest in automated alerts that surface anomalies. If you manage multiple sites, you might build pattern libraries showing how issues manifest differently across properties.

The framework is loose because your constraints are unique. What isn't negotiable: pausing between noticing and reacting, and grounding recommendations in evidence instead of instinct.

Data-driven decision-making doesn't just prevent wasted effort. It builds credibility. When stakeholders see you diagnose calmly and accurately, they trust your recommendations. When they see you admit uncertainty and test hypotheses, they respect your honesty. When your fixes actually work, they give you more autonomy.

But diagnosis only gets you so far if execution fails. You can identify the right problem and still create new ones through sloppy implementation. That's where technical precision comes in—the habit that ensures your work doesn't break the moment it touches production.

HABIT 3: TECHNICAL PRECISION

WHY TECHNICAL PROBLEMS HIDE UNTIL IT'S TOO LATE

Many technical SEO failures don't announce themselves. They accumulate quietly, in the background, while everyone assumes someone else is paying attention.

I've seen canonical templates silently break across thousands of product pages because a single variable changed in a shared component. I've watched JavaScript behave flawlessly in Chrome while failing consistently in Google's rendering environment. I've seen structured data pass every validator yet still confuse entity interpretation because the relationships weren't explicit enough. I've seen redirect chains grow one migration at a time until a simple URL required six hops to resolve. I've seen international sites where hreflang tags contradicted canonicals so badly that indexing decisions became effectively random.

None of these issues happened on amateur sites. They happened on sites run by smart, experienced teams. The common thread wasn't incompetence—it was assumption. Someone believed the foundation was stable because it had always been stable.

Technical precision is the habit of refusing to assume.

THE MOMENT WHEN VERIFICATION BECAME NONNEGOTIABLE

Early in my career, I treated technical SEO as something you investigated **after** rankings dropped. That approach worked just often enough to feel justified, and failed often enough to damage credibility.

What changed wasn't a new tool or a better crawler. It was a behavioral shift. I stopped trusting that "it should be fine" meant anything. I started verifying before problems became visible.

The habit didn't arrive all at once. It formed through small, almost invisible routines: opening Search Console before email, scanning crawl stats before meetings, spot-checking templates after deployments, even when no one asked. None of these checks felt urgent in the moment. Every one of them later prevented a much larger problem.

Verification stopped feeling like extra work and became the baseline—the minimum standard for keeping a site healthy.

WHAT ROUTINE LOOKS LIKE IN THE REAL WORLD

Technical precision only survives if it fits into real workloads. No one has time for constant deep audits, especially when juggling clients, internal stakeholders, or multiple properties.

For me, it settled into a simple rhythm. Early in the week, I scan for **changes**, not explanations. Crawl behavior might have shifted. New error categories appear. Index coverage anomalies show up. Performance metrics drift just enough to be noticeable. I don't diagnose immediately—I note what changed and when.

That small act buys time. It creates space to ask better questions before anyone panics or starts guessing.

When something looks off, the next step is never "fix SEO." It's talking to the people closest to the change. Developers know what shipped. Product teams know what moved. Content teams know what was updated. Technical precision depends less on tools and more on conversations that happen early enough to matter.

HOW COLLABORATION ACTUALLY PREVENTS BREAKAGE

For a long time, I thought collaboration meant clearly explaining SEO requirements. What it really means is staying close enough to other teams that you hear about changes before they land.

The most productive technical relationships I've had weren't built on long documents or rigid processes. They were built on short, consistent check-ins where everyone knew what was coming next.

When you regularly hear about upcoming deployments, you start spotting risks early. A new filter introduces URL parameters. A performance improvement adds aggressive lazy loading. A CMS upgrade changes URL logic without warning. None of these are mistakes—they're normal trade-offs made without SEO context unless you're present.

The goal isn't to dictate solutions. It's to surface consequences early enough that better choices are still available.

CASE STUDY—WHEN VERIFICATION SAVED A NEWS PUBLISHER

A regional news publisher with a limited budget saw their rankings collapse almost overnight. The home page fell from page one to page five. Articles followed. Internally, people were confused. A CMS upgrade had just gone live, but performance scores had improved, so no one suspected it.

The Diagnostic Path

First check: What changed recently? The CMS upgrade was deployed three days before the drop.

Second check: How was Google rendering the pages? Headlines loaded. Article bodies didn't. The content existed for users, but not for indexing.

The cause: A lazy-loading change was timing out in Google's rendering environment. The new code worked perfectly in every browser test but failed in Googlebot's JavaScript execution window.

The fix: A short call and two screenshots—what users saw versus what Google saw. The developer recognized the issue immediately and adjusted the lazy-loading threshold.

Recovery: Indexing resumed within a week. Rankings returned within three weeks.

What This Taught

The conversation worked because it was grounded in evidence and respect. I didn't prescribe a fix. I showed the impact. The solution came from development. Verification made the difference.

INSTITUTIONAL MEMORY WORKS BETTER THAN TOOLS

Most teams relearn the same technical lessons over and over. Someone leaves. A platform updates. Six months later, the same issue reappears as if it were new.

The most effective technical habit I've seen is simple documentation. At two workplaces, we used Confluence—not for long reports, but for short entries capturing what broke, why it broke, and how it was fixed.

Those notes save time. They prevent repeated mistakes. They help new team members understand weak points without discovering them the hard way. They also change how developers perceive SEO. When you bring historical context rather than vague concern, conversations become collaborative rather than defensive.

Technical precision compounds when lessons outlive the person who learned them.

DIFFERENT ENVIRONMENTS, SAME DISCIPLINE

Agency work forces skepticism. You rarely have full access. You rely on partial data and secondhand explanations. That limitation sharpens pattern recognition. You learn to ask better questions earlier and to get commitments in writing before work begins.

In-house work introduces the opposite risk. Familiarity breeds assumption. You think you know how the system works because you've lived with it for years. Meanwhile, plugins update, dependencies shift, and someone modifies a template without telling you. Verification matters most when you're confident.

Managing multiple properties introduces scale pressure. Standardization helps, but only to a point. Each site develops quirks. The habit is knowing what's shared and what's unique—and documenting the difference before it bites you.

The environment changes. The discipline does not.

BUILDING THIS HABIT

If you want to make technical precision stick, here's what tends to work:

Create a weekly verification routine. Monday mornings, scan Search Console for new errors, index coverage shifts, and crawl stat changes. Don't diagnose yet—note what looks different. This catches issues while they're still small.

Spot-check after every deployment. Pick 5-10 representative URLs across different templates. Check rendering, canonicals, structured data, and internal links. Takes 10 minutes. Prevents disasters.

Document recurring issues. Keep a simple log: what broke, why, and how it was fixed. Review it before migrations or platform changes. This becomes institutional memory that survives personnel changes.

Build relationships before you need them. Attend sprint planning. Join dev standups occasionally. Have coffee with the platform team. Play table tennis with others in the break room. When you need to flag a risk, you're not a stranger.

Test in Google's environment, not just browsers. Use Search Console's URL Inspection tool to see what Googlebot actually renders. Mobile-Friendly Test and Rich Results Test show you what systems see, not what looks good in Chrome.

Your approach depends on your access and constraints. If you're agency-side without dev access, your routine might focus on monitoring tools and clear documentation of what you're seeing. If you're in-house with full access, you might embed yourself in the deployment process. If you manage multiple sites, you might build templates for common checks.

The framework is flexible because every environment is different. What doesn't change: verify before trusting, document what breaks, and catch issues before they scale.

Technical precision doesn't prevent every SEO problem. But it prevents the avoidable ones. The canonical errors. The rendering failures. The redirect chains. The structured data that quietly breaks at scale.

These aren't the sexy problems. They're the ones that damage credibility when they slip through. They're also the ones that earn trust when you catch them early.

But catching technical issues is only half the battle. You can have flawless infrastructure and still fail if the content on that infrastructure doesn't serve users well. That's where the next habit comes in—creating content that actually meets people's needs, not just what keywords demand.

HABIT 4: CONTENT WITH PURPOSE

THE 5,000-WORD ARTICLE THAT NOBODY READ

One of the most common early-career mistakes in SEO is assuming that comprehensive content always wins. If competitors publish 1,500 words, you publish 3,000. If they publish 3,000, you go to 5,000 and call it definitive.

I did exactly that.

The article covered every angle of a complex topic. Every sub-question. Every edge case. It was thorough, accurate, and exhausting. The finished piece weighed in at just over 5,200 words.

It ranked on page two.

Average time on page: 47 seconds. Bounce rate: 84 percent.

Meanwhile, a competitor's article—about 800 words long—ranked in position three and stayed there. Month after month, stable. When I actually read it, the difference was obvious.

Their article answered the specific question people were asking in the first two paragraphs. Clear guidance. Clear next steps. My article buried the answer somewhere around word 1,200, after extensive context-setting that nobody asked for.

That was the moment I learned that comprehensiveness is not the same thing as usefulness. Purpose matters more than volume.

WHAT "PURPOSE" REALLY MEANS IN PRACTICE

Content with purpose starts with a simple question, but one many teams skip:

What is the person searching this query trying to accomplish?

Not what keyword you want to rank for. Not what topic you want to cover. Those are inputs. Purpose is the outcome the user is aiming for.

When someone searches "best running shoes for flat feet," they're trying to make a safe purchase decision and avoid discomfort or injury.

When someone searches "laptop won't turn on," they want the problem fixed quickly, without needing deep technical knowledge.

When someone searches "Mediterranean diet breakfast ideas," they're looking for realistic inspiration that fits their routine.

Each of those goals demands a different structure, tone, and depth. Once you understand that, content stops being an SEO artifact and starts becoming a tool.

PURPOSE CHANGES ACROSS THE INTENT SPECTRUM

User search intent is not binary. It moves along a spectrum, and content fails most often when it assumes every reader is at the same stage.

Early-stage research: A search like "What is estate planning?" signals curiosity and uncertainty. The reader needs orientation, plain language, and reassurance that the topic is manageable.

Mid-stage evaluation: A search like "estate planning lawyer vs. DIY estate planning" signals comparison. The reader wants trade-offs, risks, and help deciding what fits their situation.

Late-stage decision: A search like "estate planning lawyer Chicago downtown" signals urgency. The reader wants credentials, proximity, and a clear next step.

I worked with a professional services firm that treated all three stages the same way. They published dozens of educational articles that assumed no prior knowledge. The problem was that most of their organic traffic came from people already ready to hire.

Those users landed on content that talked down to them. They bounced. They hired competitors.

When the firm created decision-stage pages—specific services, clear credentials, visible outcomes—organic conversion rates increased by 40 percent in three months. Nothing magical changed. The content met people where they were.

STRUCTURE IS HOW PURPOSE BECOMES USABLE

Once you know the user's goal, structure becomes the most important decision you make.

Most SEO content fails here. It buries the answer. It forces readers to work for relevance. It follows "best practices" instead of human logic.

The inverted pyramid approach changed how I write entirely. Start with what matters most. Deliver the answer early. Add context and nuance afterward for readers who want to go deeper.

When someone searches for "best running shoes for flat feet," they shouldn't have to read 1,400 words about shoe history before seeing a recommendation. If they want that depth, they can scroll. If they don't, they should still leave satisfied.

The information doesn't change. The order does. That order determines whether the content works.

WRITING CLEARLY ENOUGH FOR HUMANS AND AI

The rise of AI-mediated search adds another layer, reinforcing the same principle rather than replacing it.

AI systems retrieve content that is easy to extract, interpret, and cite. That tends to align with content that humans also find clear.

In practice, that means:

- Lead with complete, factual statements rather than building up slowly

- Make relationships explicit rather than implied
- Use consistent terminology for the same concept
- Define people, organizations, and concepts clearly when they first appear

This is not about writing for machines. It's about removing ambiguity. Clear writing travels better—through search engines, AI systems, and human readers alike.

ESCAPING THE KEYWORD-FIRST TRAP

I've reviewed hundreds of content briefs that started with a keyword list and worked outward from there. The result is usually stiff, unnatural content that satisfies a spreadsheet but not a reader.

The strongest briefs I've seen start with purpose instead. They describe what the reader needs to decide, fix, or understand. Keywords surface naturally because the content answers real questions.

When writers know the outcome they're aiming for, the content improves immediately. Engagement improves. And counterintuitively, rankings often do too—because users actually use the content.

CASE STUDY—THE KNOWLEDGE BASE NOBODY USED

One SaaS company had an immaculate knowledge base. Every feature documented. Everything accurate. Support tickets kept increasing.

The Problem

Users weren't asking feature questions. They were asking task questions.

The documentation was organized around the product. Users were thinking in terms of problems they needed to solve.

The Diagnostic Path

Pattern in support tickets: Same questions appeared repeatedly, even though documentation existed.

User testing: Five users were asked to complete basic tasks. All struggled to find relevant help articles. They searched using task language ("how do I export my data"), but articles were titled with feature language ("Data Export Module Overview").

The mismatch: Content was comprehensive but unusable because it didn't match how people thought.

The Fix

Add a task-based layer that started with user goals and linked to deeper documentation when needed. "How do I…" articles that walked through common workflows, then pointed to feature docs for advanced users.

Support tickets dropped. Satisfaction increased. The deep documentation remained—but only for the users who actually wanted it.

Coverage didn't change. Purpose did.

WHEN CONTENT NEEDS UPDATING—AND WHEN IT DOESN'T

Content drift is real. Articles accumulate tangents, outdated examples, and unnecessary sections. The mistake is treating every decline as a freshness problem.

At a B2B software company with more than 200 articles, we evaluated content based on purpose rather than age. Some articles needed only light updates. Others needed tightening. Some no longer matched what users were searching for at all.

A small percentage were no longer worth keeping. Redirecting and retiring them improved overall site transparency.

Purpose-driven updates focus on renewed usefulness, not cosmetic signals.

BUILDING THIS HABIT

If you want to make content with purpose stick, here's what tends to work:

Start every brief with user intent, not keywords. Write one sentence describing what the user is trying to accomplish. Then write the content that accomplishes it. Keywords emerge naturally when you're solving real problems.

Use the inverted pyramid. Lead with the answer. Add supporting detail for those who want it. Respect readers who came for speed and readers who came for depth.

Test the structure before writing. Outline your content with headers that form a complete story on their own. If someone only read the headers, would they understand your answer? If not, restructure.

Match content type to the intent stage. Educational content for early research. Comparison content for evaluation. Decision-focused content for late-stage users. Don't force educational content on people ready to buy.

Audit existing content by asking: "Does this still serve its purpose?" Not "Is this outdated?" but "Would someone searching this topic today find this useful?" If no, update or retire.

Your approach depends on your content volume and team structure. If you're in-house with limited resources, focus on high-traffic pages first. If you're agency-side managing multiple clients, create purpose-first brief templates. If you have a content team, train them to think in outcomes rather than word counts.

The framework is loose because constraints vary. What doesn't change: content should accomplish something specific, and structure should make that accomplishment easy.

Content with purpose is not a tactic. It's a service. When you internalize that, your work becomes more effective, more durable, and easier to defend—regardless of how search interfaces continue to change.

But creating purposeful content is only part of the equation. You can write the perfect answer to the right question and still lose users if the experience around that content creates friction. That's where user focus comes in—the habit of noticing and removing the obstacles that stand between arrival and accomplishment.

HABIT 5: RELENTLESS USER FOCUS

THE BUTTON THAT NOBODY COULD FIND

An e-commerce client had excellent traffic and strong rankings across their primary product categories, yet conversion rates were far lower than expected. The team kept pushing for more keywords and more visibility. From their perspective, traffic was the problem.

Session recordings told a different story. Users landed on product pages, scrolled for several screens, hesitated, scrolled again, and then left. Very few reached the point where they could take action.

The add-to-cart button was technically present. It sat at the bottom of a page more than three thousand pixels long, buried beneath marketing copy, testimonials, specifications, and comparison tables. On a mobile browser, the button appeared only after several full-screen scrolls.

Users arrived ready to buy. Many never discovered how.

When the primary purchase information and the add-to-cart action were moved higher on the page, conversion rates increased noticeably within a few weeks. Rankings stayed the same. Traffic stayed the same. The experience changed.

Search visibility brought people to the page. User focus determined whether anything happened next.

WHAT USER FOCUS LOOKS LIKE WHEN YOU PRACTICE IT

Relentless user focus shows up in the questions you ask while making decisions. It shows up in moments where the data says something is "working," but users behave as if it isn't.

Pages can rank well while quietly failing at their real job. Users hesitate, abandon, or back out, even when nothing appears broken on the surface.

Practicing user focus means paying attention to friction that doesn't appear on dashboards. It means watching how real people move through pages and noticing where momentum stalls.

When teams build for rankings alone, they often mistake visibility for success. User focus corrects that mistake by grounding decisions in outcomes rather than assumptions.

WHEN SEARCH QUERIES MASK THE REAL NEED

Users rarely search in complete sentences that describe their situation. They compress their needs into short phrases and hope the result understands what they're trying to accomplish.

Someone searching "**SQL query slow**" might want a conceptual explanation—or they might be under pressure to fix a report before a meeting. The words alone don't tell you which.

Pages that focus narrowly on explaining concepts often miss the moment where users are looking for relief. In practice, many people arrive with a task in mind rather than a desire to learn.

When content aligns with the task users are trying to complete, engagement improves quickly. Pages that frame answers around outcomes tend to hold attention longer and guide users forward rather than leaving them stuck.

NAVIGATION AS SILENT FRICTION

Navigation problems rarely announce themselves. They surface through hesitation, backtracking, and abandonment.

Menus filled with internal jargon slow users down. Overloaded mega-menus overwhelm. Inconsistent behavior makes outcomes unpredictable. When users cannot tell what will happen after a click, they pause.

Simple tests expose these issues quickly. Asking someone unfamiliar with a site to find pricing or support often reveals confusion within seconds. Each extra click compounds uncertainty.

Clear navigation reduces decision fatigue and keeps users oriented. When structure makes sense, users move forward with confidence.

PERFORMANCE AS FELT EXPERIENCE

Users experience performance issues, including delays, instability, and interruptions. They notice when pages hesitate before loading content or shift unexpectedly while they're reading.

Metrics help diagnose causes, but frustration appears long before a report is reviewed. Pages can meet performance thresholds while still feeling slow or unreliable in practice.

When performance conversations focus on what users experience, prioritization becomes clearer. Fixes target the moments where attention is lost rather than abstract scores.

ACCESSIBILITY AS A SIGNAL, NOT A CHECKBOX

Accessibility issues often manifest as usability problems long before they become compliance risks. When navigation cannot be reached with the keyboard or the focus order is confusing, many users silently struggle.

Accessibility improvements tend to benefit more people than expected. A clear heading structure helps screen-reader users and visual scanners. Keyboard navigation supports users with mobility limitations and power users alike. Strong contrast improves readability in poor lighting and on mobile screens.

Treating accessibility as part of everyday user-experience work uncovers friction that analytics rarely capture. It also aligns naturally with how search systems interpret structure and definition

CASE STUDY—THE FORM THAT EXPLAINED EVERYTHING

A bank's request form saw most users abandon before submission. Session recordings of a test panel showed repeated failure points rather than overall resistance.

The Problems

Users struggled with:

- Autocomplete restrictions that prevented common input patterns
- Rigid input formats (phone numbers requiring exact formatting)
- Confusing required field indicators
- Error messages that appeared out of view on mobile screens
- Multi-step process that wasn't visible

The Fix

Adjustments focused on how people interacted with the form rather than reducing the amount of information collected. Fields remained. Interaction improved.

- Relaxed input formatting (accepts multiple phone number formats, clean server-side)
- Made required fields visually obvious before users encountered errors
- Moved error messages into view on mobile

- Added progress indicator showing steps remaining
- Enabled autocomplete where it helped instead of blocking it

The Result

Completion rates rose sharply once friction was removed from the process. The form's content didn't change. The experience did.

MOBILE CHANGES THE RULES QUIETLY

Mobile users arrive with different constraints. Smaller screens compress information. Touch interactions require space and forgiveness. Attention is fragmented, and interruptions are common.

Pages designed primarily for desktop often force mobile users to scroll excessively to reach key information. Navigation hides behind collapsed menus, and forms become difficult to complete.

When content hierarchy is reorganized with mobile constraints in mind, engagement improves even when nothing else changes. Essential information appears earlier. Actions become reachable. Sessions feel shorter and more productive.

Mobile behavior reveals where the user's focus is working—and where it breaks down.

BUILDING THIS HABIT

If you want to make user focus stick, here's what tends to work:

Watch real sessions regularly. Pick 5-10 random sessions weekly and watch how people actually use your site. Look for hesitation, backtracking, and abandonment. This reveals friction that metrics hide.

Test with outsiders. Ask someone unfamiliar with your site to complete a basic task: find pricing, contact support, or complete a purchase. Don't help. Watch where they struggle. Those moments show gaps in transparency.

Audit mobile experience separately. Don't assume desktop structure works on mobile. Load key pages on a phone and scroll through them. If critical actions require excessive scrolling or precision tapping, reorganize.

Check accessibility with keyboard navigation. Unplug your mouse. Navigate your site using only Tab, Enter, and Arrow keys. If you can't reach everything easily, neither can many users.

Map user paths from search to action. Pick your top 10 landing pages. For each, identify what users need to accomplish and whether the page makes that easy; if the path requires guesswork, redesign.

Your approach depends on your tools and access. If you're agency-side, use free tools like Hotjar or Microsoft Clarity for session recordings. If you're in-house with a budget, invest in real user monitoring. If you manage multiple sites, build a checklist of common friction points and audit systematically.

The framework is flexible because every site serves different users. What doesn't change: users reveal truth when you watch them, and friction compounds faster than you think.

User focus doesn't just improve conversion rates; it also improves the overall user experience. It changes how you think about success. Visibility becomes a means, not an end. Rankings become a signal, not a goal. The real measure becomes whether people accomplish what they came to do.

But even the best user experience can't succeed without the right kind of attention from the broader web. Authority and visibility don't appear because your site deserves them. They're earned through strategic, credible link building—the next habit, and one of the most misunderstood disciplines in SEO.

HABIT 6: STRATEGIC LINK BUILDING

THE LINKS THEY DIDN'T ASK FOR

One of the earliest lessons in SEO that stays with you comes from watching effort fail. You can spend months planning outreach, crafting polite emails, and building lists of "prospects," only to end up with a handful of weak links that never move the needle. Then, almost by accident, something else happens. A piece of work you created for your own understanding starts getting cited without any prompting. No pitch. No follow-up. Just links appearing because someone found it useful.

I first saw this clearly while reviewing a case study in sustainable building. The work wasn't created to attract attention. It was a detailed comparison of building material costs across regions, compiled to answer a real question the team kept encountering. Within a couple of months, it had been cited by industry publications, academic researchers, and trade associations. More authoritative links appeared in a few weeks than in an entire year of outreach.

The contrast was uncomfortable, but it was also clarifying. The best links weren't the ones we chased. They were the ones we earned by being genuinely useful.

WHY MOST LINK BUILDING FEELS SO HARD

Many link-building efforts struggle because they begin with the wrong question. Instead of asking what might genuinely help someone, the starting point is often a numerical target. You need links, so you work backward and try to manufacture something that looks "linkable."

The result is familiar: oversized guides that repeat what already exists, resources built to impress algorithms rather than people, and content that feels promotional the moment you land on it.

You see the pattern repeat across industries. A "comprehensive guide" is published, hundreds of outreach emails go out, and almost nobody responds. The few links that do arrive tend to come from sites that link to anything. Time is spent, effort is exhausted, and very little changes.

When you compare that to work that gets discovered organically and cited because it actually helps someone do their job, the difference is stark.

Strategic link building doesn't start with links. It starts with value—and then it waits.

WHAT PEOPLE ACTUALLY CHOOSE TO CITE

After you've watched enough content fail to attract attention, your standards change. You start asking yourself uncomfortable questions before investing in something new.

Would you cite this yourself if it appeared on another site? Would it help you explain something, support a claim, or save you time?

If the honest answer is no, it's unlikely anyone else will feel differently.

The work that **does** earn links tends to share a few traits:

- It introduces information that didn't previously exist in that form—original data, firsthand insight, or a new synthesis.
- It makes a complicated topic understandable in a way others haven't.
- It challenges a comfortable assumption, but only when there's evidence to support the challenge.

What these pieces have in common is that they remain useful even if search engines disappeared tomorrow. Their value isn't dependent on ranking.

RELATIONSHIPS THAT OUTLAST CAMPAIGNS

The most durable links rarely come from one-off tactics. They come from being known by the people who write, publish, and research in your space. Journalists, analysts, and educators remember who helps them do their work better. That recognition can't be rushed, and it doesn't respond well to pressure.

I've seen clients push for "quick wins" in link acquisition, only to become frustrated when nothing materializes. In contrast, teams that quietly spend time reading relevant coverage, contributing thoughtful insights, and answering questions without self-promotion tend to surface later as trusted sources.

Months may pass before the first citation appears. When it does, it often opens the door to others. Links arrive without pitching because credibility has been established.

The compounding effect is slow—but it's real.

WHEN DIGITAL PR ACTUALLY WORKS

Outreach has a poor reputation because so much of it is transparently self-serving. Journalists can recognize a template instantly, and they ignore it just as quickly. What they respond to is material that helps them tell a better story.

Data that reveals something unexpected. Context that clarifies a confusing development. Visualizations that make complexity easier to communicate.

I once watched a healthcare company handle this well. They had conducted a large survey about how people research medical information online. Instead of publishing a generic blog post, they examined the data for findings that challenged assumptions. They summarized those findings clearly and made the full methodology available without conditions.

When they contacted journalists who already covered digital health, the message was simple: **Here is something interesting you may want to know about.**

Several articles followed, each citing the research. No links were demanded—yet links appeared.

CASE STUDY—RESEARCH AS A LONG-TERM ASSET

A B2B software company decided to stop talking and start measuring. Their market was crowded with opinions but light on evidence.

The Approach

They invested in rigorous research on a question their industry argued about constantly but never measured: how companies actually evaluate software vendors in practice, not in theory.

The survey covered 1,200 decision-makers. The methodology was transparent. The findings contradicted several common assumptions about B2B buying.

The Results

Publications cited the data because there was nowhere else to get it. Conferences invited them to speak because the research reframed industry conversations. Competitors referenced their findings in their own content. Years later, the same study continued to be cited.

What This Taught

The links were valuable, but they weren't the main outcome. The real shift was how the company was perceived. They became a source rather than a vendor.

That distinction outlived the campaign and reshaped their visibility across channels.

AUTHORITY TRAVELS WITH THE SOURCE

Links and perceived authority reinforce each other. When a brand or individual is clearly recognized as a distinct entity, citations come more easily. Names are used consistently. Mentions are more likely to be linked automatically. Content is treated as a reference point rather than a marketing asset.

This matters not only for traditional search but also for how newer systems surface and summarize information.

I've seen organizations struggle simply because they were difficult to identify. Inconsistent naming, weak profiles, and unclear attribution made them harder to cite. Once those issues were corrected, journalists found them more easily, mentions turned into links, and their work began appearing in broader summaries.

The links didn't create coherence about the entity. The coherence created the links.

TACTICS THAT AGE POORLY

Some approaches persist because they promise speed, even though they rarely deliver lasting value. Writing solely for author-bio links, paying for editorial-style placements, or participating in obvious exchange networks might produce short-term gains—but they also leave patterns that are hard to defend.

A useful rule of thumb: If you would hesitate to explain how a link was acquired to a peer you respect, it's probably not worth pursuing.

The reputational cost often outweighs the temporary benefit.

BUILDING THIS HABIT

If you want to make strategic link building stick, here's what tends to work:

Create assets worth referencing. Original research, useful tools, clear data visualizations, or explanations that become the default reference. Ask yourself: would I cite this if someone else published it?

Build relationships before you need them. Follow journalists and researchers in your space. Share their work. Contribute thoughtfully when you have genuine expertise. Be helpful without expecting immediate return.

Make methodology transparent. If you publish data, show how you gathered it. If you make claims, cite sources. Transparency builds trust, and trust creates citations.

Help journalists do their job. When you have genuine expertise on a developing story, offer context without pitching. Journalists remember sources who make their work easier.

Measure what matters. Track referring domains, but also track who's citing you, in what context, and whether those sources align with your credibility goals. Quality compounds differently from quantity.

Your approach depends on resources and industry. If you're in-house with research capabilities, invest in original data. If you're agency-side, focus on relationship-building and content that solves real problems. If you're in a technical field, create tools or resources that practitioners actually use.

The framework is loose because markets value different things. What doesn't change: earn links by being useful, and build relationships that outlast individual campaigns.

Strategic link building is often misunderstood as "playing safe." I see it as choosing foundations that don't collapse when the environment gets stricter. It protects your work from constant cleanup, aligns you with how search systems evaluate credibility, and builds authority that continues to attract attention long after the original effort.

But even the strongest link profile won't save you when the ground shifts beneath your feet. Algorithm updates, interface changes, and market disruptions arrive without warning. That's where adaptability comes in—the habit of absorbing change without losing your footing.

HABIT 7: ADAPTABILITY TO CHANGE

PANIC CAN KILL SEO

You can tell when something shifts in search because the industry starts sounding like a fire alarm. A graph drops, a thread explodes, and people start explaining what happened before anyone has looked at the data. Within hours, there are confident explanations for outcomes nobody has had time to measure.

Most of the costly mistakes I've seen around updates didn't originate in the update itself. They originated in the response. When people get anxious, they start seeing patterns where none exist. They start "fixing" pages that aren't broken. They change multiple variables at once, which makes it impossible to learn what actually happened.

A few days later, when the dust settles, you're left with a mess: a blurred baseline, a confused story, and a set of changes you can't confidently defend.

There's a particular kind of pressure that comes with being responsible for traffic. You feel accountable and watched, with an urge to move. That urge can turn a manageable fluctuation into a self-inflicted incident. Years in, you stop treating volatility as a personal accusation. You treat it as system behavior that needs time and context before it deserves a response.

NAMING THE CHANGE BEFORE YOU CHASE IT

A traffic drop is a symptom. The hard part is that very different causes can look identical in a dashboard. That's why adaptable SEOs slow down and ask, "What kind of change is this?" They do it before they write a single brief, send a single dev ticket, or touch a template.

Sometimes demand shifts, and the "loss" is fewer people searching. Sometimes a competitor publishes something strong and steadily pushes you down. Sometimes you approve something that changes rendering or indexing signals, and you only notice once the crawl and index data catch up. Sometimes rankings hold, but clicks drop because the results page now answers the question before users need to click.

This habit isn't a framework you print and tape to your monitor. It shows up as a tone in the room. Instead of "we got hit," you hear "let's isolate what moved first." Instead of rewriting pages on day one, someone checks recent releases, segments performance, compares affected templates, and looks at the search results page itself.

UNDERSTANDING RANKING VS. RETRIEVAL

The systems evolve, the interfaces shift, and the outputs change shape. The discipline continues. You're still trying to make information easier to discover, easier to trust, and easier to use.

One distinction is helpful in the current era: ranking and retrieval are related but **distinct behaviors.**

Ranking is ordering within a list. Retrieval is the system's decision about what to pull from the index, what to summarize, and which sources to cite.

The difference matters because it changes what "visibility" looks like. It also changes what you should measure.

CASE STUDY—THE EXPENSIVE FIX THAT TAUGHT EVERYONE TO WAIT

A client saw rankings slide during a period when the industry was already on edge. The first recommendations floating around were dramatic: rewrite a large chunk of the site, restructure sections, overhaul internal linking, "refresh" everything. The plan sounded decisive, which is exactly why it was tempting.

The team slowed down. They captured the state of key pages and queries, then watched what happened across the following days. The rollout settled. Rankings returned. The drop was part of the recalibration churn, not a permanent verdict on the site.

That pause saved weeks of work and a budget that would have been swallowed by activity that delivered no learning. It also changed how the client behaved during subsequent wobbles. They learned to separate movement from meaning, and to treat early volatility as provisional.

CASE STUDY—THE PROBLEM WASN'T ABOUT RANKING

Another case looked like a standard visibility loss until someone bothered to look at the results page.

A healthcare site appeared to lose meaningful traffic for informational queries. The instinctive story was predictable: an update reduced trust in the pages. The numbers were real, but the story didn't fit. There were no clear signs of a broad update, peers weren't reporting similar collapses, and the site's technical signals held steady.

What had changed was the interface. AI-generated summaries began appearing more frequently for those queries, taking prime space and satisfying more users without a click. Positions didn't collapse. Click behavior did.

When you misread that scenario as a ranking problem, you can spend months "improving quality" while the underlying mechanism is elsewhere. The adaptation is different. You watch whether your pages get cited. You adjust how clearly the page states key facts and definitions. You build deeper content for the moments when users still need something beyond the summary. You also accept that some click loss is structural and permanent, and you stop treating it as a temporary malfunction.

HOLDING STEADY IS PART OF THE JOB

SEO culture rewards action. Waiting can look like passivity, especially when stakeholders want reassurance. The people who handle change well get comfortable saying, "I don't know yet," while they gather enough evidence to form a credible theory. They also protect their baseline. They avoid changing ten things at once because they know what that destroys: the ability to learn.

You start treating your site like an environment where cause and effect matter. You want stable conditions for measurement. You want changes you can explain and defend. You want to preserve the difference between what the system did and what you did.

WHEN YOU DO NEED TO MOVE

There are moments where speed matters. They usually show up as confirmed technical failure, not as industry panic.

When something breaks—rendering, canonicals, indexing directives, analytics instrumentation—the right move is to get methodical quickly. You look at recent releases. You validate what changed between the source and the rendering. You compare crawl and index behavior. You check whether the issue is isolated to a template, section, device class, or geography. You aim for a clean diagnosis because a clean diagnosis produces a clean fix.

Other situations are strategic and slower. A competitor raises the quality bar in your niche and steadily pushes you down. There's no single day you can point to. It just becomes harder to win. The response is targeted improvement in areas that matter, informed by what users and systems are rewarding now. That work is rarely dramatic. It's steady, careful, and cumulative.

THE AI SHIFT AS A FAMILIAR KIND OF PROBLEM

Artificial intelligence has changed how many people encounter information, and it has changed what "success" feels like. You can do good work and still watch click-through rates soften for certain query classes. The explanation is often interface-driven. People get answers earlier. They still see brands. They click less.

When featured snippets expanded, SEOs learned to write and structure content so it could be extracted cleanly. When rich results grew, we learned to align markup, page intent, and template hygiene. AI-mediated retrieval pushes those same instincts further.

Factual accuracy matters. Attribution matters. Entity consistency matters. Sources matter. Extractability matters.

The work stays recognizable. What shifts is the surface area where visibility happens.

BUILDING THIS HABIT

If you want to make adaptability stick, here's what tends to work:

Create a change timeline. Keep a simple log of deployments, content releases, migrations, and industry updates. When performance shifts, you have context to work from rather than guess.

Isolate before diagnosing. When something moves, ask: What changed? When did it start? Where is it concentrated? What shape does it have? Answer these before prescribing fixes.

Protect your baseline. Avoid changing multiple variables during volatility. You need clean data to learn from. One change at a time, with clear before/after measurement.

Distinguish interface changes from ranking changes. Check the actual SERP. If AI summaries, featured snippets, or other elements have changed, you're dealing with click redistribution, not ranking loss.

Build stakeholder patience. Explain what you expect to see during normal volatility vs. what would signal real problems. Set expectations early that not all movement requires action.

Your approach depends on your role. If you're agency-side, educate clients on typical post-update behavior. If you're in-house, build internal dashboards that separate noise from signal. If you manage multiple sites, document how each property typically responds to industry shifts.

The framework is loose because every situation is unique. What doesn't change: pause before reacting, protect your ability to learn, and respond from evidence rather than urgency.

Adaptability doesn't mean you never react—it means you react from understanding rather than fear. When you can sit inside volatility without adding to it, you make better decisions. You also build trust with stakeholders by staying calm when others are scrambling.

But adaptability alone won't help you if you're working in isolation. SEO work rarely ships without support from other teams. That's where collaboration comes in—the habit of working across disciplines without creating friction that slows everything down.

HABIT 8: COLLABORATION WITHOUT FRICTION

SHOWING BEATS TELLING

There is a particular kind of resistance that data alone does not dissolve. You can present the analysis, outline search intent, and walk through the logic, yet still hear, "That's how our industry does it," or, "Users don't care about that," or, "We've always done it this way."

One of the fastest ways through that wall is to observe real user behavior together.

I've been in rooms where teams spent weeks debating whether product specs should sit higher on the page, whether comparison tools were visible enough, or whether navigation was confusing. Then someone opened a few session recordings. Ten users. Thirty minutes. You could watch people scroll past key content, hesitate, hunt for details, open multiple tabs, and abandon the page entirely.

The shift in the conversation was immediate because the problem stopped being theoretical. Nobody needed convincing. They had seen it.

Collaboration improves when you make the problem visible without turning it into an argument.

CASE STUDY—THE NAVIGATION REDESIGN THAT ALMOST BROKE SEARCH

At a SaaS company, the design team proposed a complete redesign of the navigation. It was the kind of work designers enjoy: new information architecture, cleaner menus, and a more coherent task flow. Early user testing looked promising.

From an SEO perspective, the proposal carried real risk. Many URLs would change, internal links would shift, internal PageRank would redistribute, and some high-performing category pages risked being buried or removed. The simplest reaction would have been to block the project with a firm, "We can't do this; it will hurt search."

That approach turns the SEO team into an obstacle rather than a partner.

The better move was to get involved early and treat the design goals as legitimate. In the review meeting, the conversation shifted from "stop" to "plan." Keep the visual improvements. Preserve URLs where possible. Where changes were unavoidable, the map redirects carefully. Roll out in phases instead of flipping the entire system at once. Monitor the impact section by section so issues can be surfaced while they are still manageable.

The result wasn't a compromise that diluted everyone's goals. It was a plan that balanced both usability and search visibility because the teams worked on the same problem rather than defending separate priorities.

DISAGREEMENT WITHOUT ENEMIES

People will disagree with you. Sometimes they'll be right. Sometimes you will. That's normal in cross-functional work. One of my sayings is, "SEO should never be the tail that wags the dog." The business objectives always come first.

One of the simplest ways to keep collaboration intact is to acknowledge constraints before you argue your case. Engineering has bandwidth limits. Product has competing priorities. Legal has genuine risk considerations. If you ignore those realities, you sound disconnected from how the organization actually works.

Another useful habit is separating data from ego. When you can point to patterns in Google Search Console, indexing behavior, or conversion impacts, disagreement becomes easier to resolve. It stops being a clash of opinions and becomes a question of what the evidence supports.

Options also travel better than ultimatums. When you offer a small, low-risk path alongside a deeper fix, teams can choose an approach that fits their reality. You still advocate for what matters, but you avoid forcing an all-or-nothing decision.

WHEN YOU ARE WRONG

Most SEOs have made recommendations they wish they could revise. Maybe you anchored on the wrong diagnosis. Maybe you pushed for a structural change that created work without a meaningful payoff. Maybe you overestimated the impact of a markup change that didn't move anything measurable.

What matters in those moments is less the error and more what happens next. People notice whether you acknowledge it quickly, explain what you learned, and adjust course without defensiveness. Nothing erodes trust faster than pretending a mistake was someone else's fault.

Your credibility becomes a record of two things: what worked, and how you behaved when something didn't.

A RHYTHM THAT PREVENTS CRISES

Friction increases when collaboration only happens during emergencies. If a developer first hears about SEO during a release incident, the relationship becomes reactive by default.

In organizations where collaboration works well, there's usually a simple cadence. Short check-ins that prevent surprises. Content conversations that happen before topics are locked in. Quarterly planning where SEO is present early enough to influence direction rather than complain after the fact. The meetings don't need to be long. They need to exist consistently.

You feel the difference immediately. Instead of fighting to be included, you become part of how work gets done.

BUILDING THIS HABIT

If you want to make collaboration stick, here's what tends to work:

Join planning early. Attend sprint planning, product roadmap sessions, or editorial calendars before decisions are locked. Early presence prevents late objections.

Make problems visible. Use session recordings, heatmaps, or Search Console data to show issues rather than describe them. People respond to what they can see.

Speak in outcomes, not tactics. Instead of "we need canonical tags," say "users are finding duplicate pages and getting confused." Translate SEO into business impact.

Document decisions. Keep a simple record of what was discussed, what was agreed, and why. This prevents circular conversations and helps new team members onboard.

Acknowledge constraints. When you make a request, show you understand bandwidth, priorities, and trade-offs. It changes how people hear your recommendations.

Your approach depends on your organization. If you're agency-side, focus on clear documentation and regular check-ins since access is limited. If you're in-house, embed yourself in other teams' processes. If you manage multiple properties, create templates that enable repeatable collaboration.

The framework is flexible because every environment is different. What doesn't change: relationships enable work, visibility beats explanation, and early involvement beats late objections.

Collaboration without friction doesn't just make your job easier—it makes your work ship. The best SEO strategies fail if they never leave the backlog. When you can work across teams smoothly, your recommendations become real changes on real sites.

But even the best collaboration breaks down without systems to support it. That's where process discipline comes in—the habit of building repeatable routines that catch mistakes before they scale.

HABIT 9: PROCESS DISCIPLINE

FORGETTING TO CHECK CANONICALS

The migration had the familiar rhythm of a team that had done this many times before. The consultant knew the steps. The timeline felt casual because the work felt routine. Questions were answered quickly. Very little was written down. Nothing about it was sloppy—it was simply confident.

Go-live happened on a Friday afternoon, which always feels harmless until it isn't. The team did the usual spot-checks. The home page loaded. A few product pages loaded. A couple of blog posts looked normal. Everyone went into the weekend with the quiet relief that comes from seeing something "work" after weeks of preparation.

Monday felt different.

Organic traffic was down 30 percent.

Search Console made the cause painfully clear. The new site was canonicalizing every page to the home page. Thousands of URLs, all pointing to one. The template's canonical logic was never validated during the final checks.

It took three days to fix. It took much longer for the recovery to feel complete.

What stays with you is how ordinary the failure was. Nobody forgot what canonicals are. Nobody dismissed their importance. The team trusted memory under pressure, and memory made a quiet decision on their behalf.

WHY PREVENTABLE MISTAKES KEEP HAPPENING

In SEO, people like to believe that expertise protects them from errors. You hear it in the confidence that comes with experience: "I've done this before," "I know what to watch," "I'll catch anything important." That confidence isn't arrogance—it's how people cope with the sheer breadth of the work.

But expertise creates its own blind spots. When something becomes familiar, you stop treating it as fragile. You rely on attention and pattern recognition. You also start compressing steps. Under deadlines, those compressions get more aggressive.

That's when small failures slip through. And the failures are usually boring: canonicals, redirects, robots directives, templated metadata, analytics tags, rendering changes you can't see without testing. These aren't complex mistakes. They're omissions. They happen because real work is noisy, and nobody operates with perfect focus.

Process discipline exists for the moments when you are tired, rushed, and confident at the same time.

BREAKAGES WHEN THE PROCESS IS MISSING

Most SEO failures don't arrive as dramatic events. They show up as drift. A migration introduces a template error. A deployment removes structured data from a section. A new script changes rendering order. Internal links accumulate into chains. Orphan pages multiply quietly. Small warning signs appear, then fade into the background.

Content drift is even easier to miss because it doesn't look like a bug. Articles get published with inconsistent baseline quality. Some pages connect cleanly into the internal linking structure. Others remain isolated. A few writers take search intent seriously. Others write as though every piece is a generic explainer. Nothing is "wrong" on any single day, but the site becomes harder to maintain and harder for systems to interpret.

Communication drift follows the same pattern. Tickets get reopened because nobody remembers what was tried. New team members repeat old mistakes because decisions live in conversations rather than in records. Work becomes reactive because the organization can't hold its own memory.

The common thread is that people believe they will remember. They believe they will notice. They believe attention will hold up even when it is least reliable.

WHEN A HABIT REPLACES A HERO MOMENT

The first time you build a process, it feels like extra work. It looks slower than just doing the task. You can feel your own impatience, especially when the fix seems obvious, and you want to move.

Then you have a week where the process catches something you would have missed. Maybe it's a redirect pointing to a staging domain. Maybe it's a canonical template that flipped. Maybe it's a robots directive left behind after a test. The problem is small—and that's the point. You catch it while it's still small.

That's when process discipline stops feeling like admin and starts feeling like protection.

You also notice something else: the process removes negotiation from recurring work. Instead of deciding every time what "good enough" looks like, you move through a known sequence. The mental load drops. The outcome becomes more consistent. Stakeholders experience that consistency as professionalism, even if they never see the checklist behind it.

HOW BASELINE QUALITY GETS MADE

I've watched teams struggle with publishing for months, convinced the problem was talent. One writer was "good," another was "not SEO-friendly," an editor kept missing internal links, someone always forgot alt text, and nobody treated updates consistently. The team tried coaching, then training, then more meetings.

The turning point was rarely a new lesson. It was a small, shared routine that defined what "done" meant.

The simplest version wasn't long. It was tied to their publishing workflow, so it couldn't be skipped without someone noticing. It covered the things that always caused rework: is the page's purpose clear, does the opening answer the query quickly, are headings meaningful, are there contextual internal links, did anything technical break during the edit, and is the mobile experience still intact?

Five minutes of deliberate checking saved hours of cleanup later. More importantly, it stopped content quality from being a matter of mood. The floor rose. That's what a well-designed process does—it creates a floor.

THE PRE-DEPLOYMENT MOMENT WHERE CAREERS GET MADE

If there's one place where process discipline pays for itself, it's in releases. Deployments are where small omissions become large problems because they scale instantly across templates and URLs.

I've seen teams treat pre-deployment verification as optional because it feels like friction when everyone is trying to ship. The teams that avoid incidents treat it as a non-negotiable pause. They don't do it because they love process. They do it because they've lived through the kind of Monday call that makes everyone question the last two months of work.

The irony is that pre-deployment checks are rarely complicated. They're specific, repeatable validations against known failure points. The challenge isn't difficulty. The challenge is consistency.

When the habit exists, it catches the quiet disasters: canonical patterns flipping, template redirects misfiring, robots directives blocking sections, sitemaps pointing at the wrong host, and structured data disappearing. None of these is dramatic until they're live.

DOCUMENTATION THAT SURVIVES REAL WORK

A lot of SEO documentation looks impressive and accomplishes nothing. It's written like a reference manual and stored like an archive. People don't read it because they're not trying to become SEOs. They're trying to ship their own work without breaking anything.

The documentation that gets used is usually small and close to the task. A short migration-mapping format that everyone can follow. A one-page release verification note that is attached to the ticket. A brief content template that makes purpose and audience unmistakable. A short list of recurring technical failures written in language engineering recognizes.

The test is simple and unforgiving: can someone use this while they're busy? If yes, it survives. If not, it becomes another file nobody opens.

BUILDING THIS HABIT

If you want to make process discipline stick, here's what tends to work:

Create a pre-deployment checklist. Five to ten items covering common failure points: canonicals, redirects, robots, structured data, internal links, and rendering. Make it mandatory before any release.

Document recurring issues. Keep a simple log: date, what broke, why, and how it was fixed. Review before migrations or major changes. This becomes institutional memory.

Build publishing templates. Define "done" for different content types. Make it part of the workflow, not an optional step. Include purpose, structure, internal links, and mobile browser check.

Automate what you can. Weekly crawls, error monitoring, and index coverage alerts. Automation doesn't solve problems, but it surfaces them before they scale.

Make documentation actionable. Short, task-focused, close to where work happens. Skip the theory. Answer: "What do I do right now?"

Your approach depends on your environment. If you're agency-side, create lightweight templates for each client. If you're in-house, embed checks into deployment pipelines. If you manage multiple sites, standardize what you can while documenting unique quirks.

The framework is flexible because every team is different. What doesn't change: catch issues before they scale, document what breaks, and remove decision fatigue from recurring work.

Process discipline isn't glamorous. It rarely earns praise on a good week because nothing goes wrong. Its value shows up in what doesn't happen: the migration that doesn't collapse, the release that doesn't break indexing, the content updates that don't remove internal links, the technical drift that gets caught early.

But process alone isn't enough if you're always operating in panic mode. You need the discipline to protect your work—and the patience to let it mature. That's where strategic patience comes in, the habit that separates people who thrive from people who burn out chasing every fluctuation.

HABIT 10: STRATEGIC PATIENCE

THE MOMENT YOU LEARN THAT SEO HAS ITS OWN CLOCK

Most operators remember the moment they realized SEO does not move at the speed of their effort. You ship a fix, publish an update, earn a strong link, and expect the graph to respond the way a human would respond: immediately, logically, and in the direction you pushed.

Then nothing happens.

Or the opposite happens. You make a change you feel confident about, and the numbers wobble. People ask what went wrong. You start second-guessing work that hasn't even had time to be interpreted. That's how operators end up in a cycle of restless adjustments—making changes, watching the line, making more changes, and losing track of what caused what.

Strategic patience is the ability to live inside that delay without filling it with panic work.

WHAT TIME FEELS LIKE WHEN YOU ARE RESPONSIBLE FOR THE NUMBERS

Patience sounds like a personality trait until you have to defend it on a Monday morning call.

Stakeholders don't ask, "What does the system need to process this change?" They ask, "Did it work?" They ask, "When will we know?" They ask, "Why is traffic still down if we fixed it?" Under that pressure, it becomes tempting to offer certainty you don't have or to add more activity so it looks like you're doing something.

Operators who last in SEO learn to manage expectations in a grounded way, even when outcomes aren't immediate. They also learn that different kinds of work mature at different speeds. A template fix tends to show its impact sooner than an authority shift. A content refresh settles differently from a new link profile. When you treat all changes as if they should behave the same way, you create false alarms and premature reversals.

THE WAITING PERIOD THAT SAVES YOU FROM YOURSELF

A common pattern in SEO is mistaking early movement for meaning. The first few days after an update or a visible shake-up are often the least reliable time to draw any conclusions. Rankings jump around. Search results change hour by hour. You can screenshot five different "realities" in one afternoon.

This is where strategic patience pays for itself. You allow enough time for patterns to hold before you decide what the story is. You gather evidence while you still have a clean baseline. You avoid the frantic, multi-variable response that turns diagnosis into guesswork.

I learned this from watching teams spend money they didn't need to spend. A client saw a drop in rankings during a volatile period and immediately moved into rewrite mode. Pages were overhauled, templates were adjusted, and the strategy was "refreshed." The work cost weeks and a meaningful budget. Two weeks later, rankings returned to where they had been. The drop belonged to rollout churn, not a permanent loss of trust. The rebuild didn't cause the recovery—it simply happened during the same window.

What stings about that story is how understandable it was. People felt responsible. People wanted control. They didn't want to sit still while something important looked broken. Strategic patience is often the skill of resisting that urge long enough to avoid doing expensive, noisy work that teaches you nothing.

THE DIFFERENCE BETWEEN "FIXABLE" AND "MATURING"

You start separating SEO work into two broad categories: things that are clearly broken and things that need time to mature.

When something is broken, the evidence is usually concrete. Pages stop being indexed. Canonicals flip. Rendering changes. Robots.txt directives block sections. Tracking disappears. Those failures call for speed and focus because waiting prolongs the damage.

Maturing work feels different. You update content so it matches how people search today. You publish a piece that should earn citations over time. You strengthen an entity footprint so systems associate your brand with a topic more consistently. These efforts rarely produce instant outcomes. They accumulate. They settle. They sometimes wobble before improving because systems re-evaluate their positioning as new signals arrive.

Strategic patience doesn't mean sitting on your hands. It means choosing the right tempo for the kind of work you're doing.

WHEN THE INTERFACE CHANGES FASTER THAN YOUR RANKINGS

A lot of modern SEO frustration comes from a mismatch between where visibility happens and what you're measuring.

You can keep rankings stable and still see traffic soften because the results page itself has changed. AI summaries, expanded features, shopping blocks, local packs, and other layouts can reduce clicks without changing your position in the list. When you treat that as a ranking problem, you end up chasing the wrong thing.

More experienced operators develop patience with the distinction. They watch whether visibility is shifting into citations, previews, and summaries. They pay attention to the brand's presence on those surfaces. They stop expecting every improvement to translate into immediate clicks, especially for informational queries where the interface now answers earlier in the journey.

They also avoid magical thinking about AI systems. Some systems retrieve live. Some rely on training cycles. You cannot force a model to "learn" your new content on your timeline. You can, however, make your work easier to cite and extract, then give the ecosystem time to pick it up where it can.

PATIENCE AS A COMPETITIVE ADVANTAGE

I've worked with teams who were obsessed with volume because their competitors were loud. The competitor published constantly, promoted everything, and seemed to dominate the conversation. The temptation was to match that pace and flood the site with content to keep up.

The teams that outlasted those competitors did something quieter. They produced fewer pieces, but each piece carried real weight. They built assets others could cite without embarrassment. They invested in technical consistency to prevent regressions from undermining their work. They let relationships form slowly rather than treating outreach as a campaign that had to "perform" in a single month.

In the early months, that approach can look unimpressive. It doesn't produce exciting weekly graphs. Over a year or two, it changes the shape of authority. Citations become easier to earn. Links show up in better places. Older content keeps pulling value forward. Meanwhile, the volume strategy often turns into maintenance debt—large libraries that need constant cleanup and deliver diminishing returns.

This is why strategic patience can feel like restraint in the short term and like dominance in the long term. You're building assets that keep working after the publishing week is over.

THE HARD PART IS DEFENDING PATIENCE WITHOUT SOUNDING VAGUE

The phrase "we need to be patient" usually fails because it sounds like stalling. It's too abstract. People hear it as, "We don't know what we're doing."

What works better is speaking in observable signals and giving people something real to watch while the larger outcome matures. You describe what you expect to see first and what would count as meaningful progress before traffic follows. You point to crawl behavior, indexing trends, impressions, ranking stability, and whether the right pages are being surfaced for the right queries. You show motion without pretending you can force the final result by next Tuesday.

That style of communication changes the dynamic. Stakeholders feel less compelled to demand a new strategy every week because they can see the system processing the work, even if the headline number hasn't shifted yet.

LEARNING THE SEASONAL LANGUAGE OF YOUR OWN SITE

Patience becomes easier when you recognize what "normal" looks like. Every site has its own cycles. Some industries soften during holidays. Some surge at quarter's end. Some respond to academic calendars. Some follow weather patterns. Some depend on annual events that reliably move demand.

When you learn those cycles, you stop treating expected drops as emergencies. You also get better at spotting anomalies because you're no longer chasing predictable noise. That saves attention for the moments when something genuinely unusual happens.

BUILDING THIS HABIT

If you want to make strategic patience stick, here's what tends to work:

Separate broken from maturing. When performance shifts, ask: Is this broken (concrete failure) or maturing (work that needs time)? Broken gets speed. Maturing gets monitoring.

Set milestone expectations. Before launching changes, write down what you expect to see first, second, and third. Share this timeline with stakeholders so they know what progression looks like.

Protect your baseline. Avoid stacking changes during uncertain periods. You need clean data to learn from. One variable at a time, with clear measurement windows.

Document your site's cycles. Track seasonal patterns, typical volatility ranges, and recovery timelines. This becomes your reference for "normal."

Communicate in observables. Instead of "be patient," say "we expect indexing to stabilize this week, then impressions to climb, then clicks to follow 2-3 weeks later."

Your approach depends on your constraints. If you're agency-side, educate clients on realistic timelines for different work types. If you're in-house, build stakeholder literacy around how search systems process changes. If you manage multiple sites, document how each property typically responds to similar interventions.

The framework is loose because every situation is unique. What doesn't change: strategic patience isn't passive—it's disciplined restraint that protects your ability to learn.

Strategic patience doesn't just prevent wasted effort. It changes how people perceive your judgment. When you can face uncertainty without reacting impulsively, stakeholders begin to trust your instincts. They stop second-guessing every fluctuation because they've seen you stay calm and be right.

But patience without principle creates a different problem. You can wait forever and still build on shaky foundations if you're not guided by ethical integrity. That's where the next habit comes in—the discipline that ensures your work can withstand scrutiny long after it's shipped.

HABIT 11: ETHICAL INTEGRITY

THE SHORTCUT CONVERSATION YOU LEARN TO RECOGNIZE

There is a moment in most SEO careers when a client leans in and lowers their voice, as though the room itself might be listening.

"I heard there's a way to do this faster."

Sometimes it's framed as curiosity. Sometimes it's frustration after watching a competitor outrank them. Sometimes it's a friend-of-a-friend recommendation wrapped in the promise of a "secret technique." The details vary, but the tone is consistent. They want something that feels edgy.

If you've been around long enough, you start hearing the question underneath the question. They're asking whether you will take on a risk they don't fully understand.

Early in my career, I treated ethics in SEO like a policy you explain. Over time, it became something else—a strategic posture. Not because it sounds noble, but because the alternative usually ends the same way: a brief period of apparent success, followed by a recovery project nobody wants to pay for, followed by a trust problem that outlasts the penalty.

Search systems keep moving toward the same goal: surfacing content that is credible, useful, and safe to show to users. When your work moves in that direction, it tends to age well. When your work depends on deception, the shelf life is always shorter than the sales pitch suggests.

THE RISK NOBODY MENTIONS WHEN THEY SELL YOU A TACTIC

People who sell manipulative tactics rarely frame them as gambling, but that's what they are. You're betting that a system designed to detect manufactured signals won't detect yours, and you're betting that the cost of being wrong will be manageable.

That second part is where most pitches quietly fall apart.

A bad bet doesn't just cost rankings; it costs careers. It can damage credibility with stakeholders, erode trust with customers, and consume time you won't get back. It can also leave a difficult-to-erase footprint. Cleanup work is rarely as simple as "remove the bad links" or "delete the low-quality pages." The after-effects linger. The reputation lingers. The internal doubt lingers.

I don't take that bet. I also don't let clients take it without understanding what they're really agreeing to.

THE TACTICS THAT ALWAYS COME UP

When someone asks about shortcuts, the same categories tend to appear. Networks of sites built solely to link to a target. Paid placements dressed up as editorial. Guest posting programs designed to scale bio links. Mass content production that exists to occupy keywords rather than answer questions. Cloaking, hidden text, and link exchanges that try to look organic while operating like a machine.

These tactics get presented as clever. They're usually predictable.

They also age poorly because they depend on patterns remaining invisible. Search systems are built to find patterns. Once a pattern becomes common, it becomes detectable. When enough people do something, it stops being a secret and starts being a fingerprint.

Even when the tactic appears to "work," it often works in a way that creates a future problem. You build a foundation that needs constant monitoring, constant cleanup, and constant anxiety. That isn't growth. That's maintenance debt.

BUILDING AUTHORITY THE SLOW WAY THAT KEEPS WORKING

The ethical path in SEO often looks boring from the outside. Hacks don't drive it. It's driven by work that others can trust.

Original research is one example. When you publish data nobody else has, citations show up because people need a source. Over time, the asset becomes something that continues to attract attention without constant promotion.

Expert positioning is another. When a technical team becomes known for transparency and accuracy, journalists start coming to them. That turns into citations that feel earned because they are. You can see the difference in the links themselves—they come from coverage, not transactions.

Tools and resources also have a different kind of gravity. A calculator that helps people do real work. A dataset people can cite. A template that saves time. A guide that explains something complex in a way that becomes the default reference. These earn links in the only way that matters long-term: people use them and refer to them.

The pattern behind all of these is simple: value first, recognition second. When you build things worth referencing, the link story becomes less stressful because it no longer relies on persuasion.

TRANSPARENCY AS A PROFESSIONAL REFLEX

Ethical integrity also shows up in how you communicate, especially when you're under pressure to promise outcomes.

There is a type of SEO pitch built on certainty—guarantees, delivery-style timelines, confident statements about results nobody can control. Clients often want that certainty because it feels safe. The trouble is that the certainty is usually theater.

Honest work looks different. You talk about what you can control and what you can't. You set expectations that reflect how search systems behave. You're clear about uncertainty. You avoid framing every recommendation as inevitable success. You also protect clients from their own optimism, especially when they're excited by a tactic they read in a headline.

This kind of communication can feel harder in the moment, but it builds a relationship that survives reality. When results arrive more slowly than hoped, you still have trust. When the market shifts, you still have credibility. That matters more than a confident promise that can't be kept.

CASE STUDY—WATCHING A COMPETITOR GET AWAY WITH IT

One of the hardest ethical moments in SEO is watching a competitor rank while doing something clearly manipulative. Clients see it. Teams see it. The question arrives quickly: why are they winning if this is "wrong"?

I've lived through enough cycles to know how that story often ends. The competitor is building on a foundation that appears stable until it isn't. Spam detection improves. A new filter lands. A pattern gets discounted. Rankings that relied on manufactured signals suddenly lose their scaffolding.

I worked with a healthcare company that watched a competitor climb on an obvious diet of bought placements and low-grade citations. Month after month, the competitor seemed to be rewarded. The client's frustration was understandable. They wanted to compete on the same terms.

We stayed on the slower path: better content, real partnerships, cleaner technical work, and assets that deserved citations. It required patience and, at times, a thick skin.

Later, a link-spam update targeted the same patterns the competitor relied on. Their visibility collapsed across the queries that mattered most. The ethical site moved up without doing anything dramatic because its foundation wasn't discounted. The client didn't need a rescue plan. They needed time.

Those moments shape your career. They teach you that "working right now" is not the same thing as "working."

ACCESSIBILITY AS PART OF INTEGRITY

Ethical SEO isn't limited to how you acquire links. It's also about who can use what you publish.

When you start paying attention to accessibility, you realize how many sites quietly exclude people. Images with meaningless alt text. Heading structures that make sense visually but collapse for screen readers. Navigation that fails without a mouse. Forms that don't communicate errors properly. Color contrast choices that look stylish but leave some users guessing.

Accessibility can be framed as compliance, and sometimes it needs to be. I tend to see it as respect and reach. When a site becomes easier to navigate and understand across different conditions, more people can use it. Search systems also tend to reward lucidity and structure, which is one reason accessibility improvements often improve the overall experience.

You don't need to turn accessibility into a slogan. You build it into the way you think about quality.

BUILDING THIS HABIT

If you want to make ethical integrity stick, here's what tends to work:

Run the transparency test. If you would hesitate to explain how a link was acquired to a peer you respect, don't pursue it. If you can't defend a tactic publicly, it's not worth the risk.

Build value-first assets. Original research, useful tools, clear visualizations, definitive guides. Ask yourself: would I cite this if someone else published it?

Set honest expectations. Talk about what you can control and what you can't. Be clear about uncertainty. Protect clients from tactics that sound good but carry hidden costs.

Document your decisions. Keep a record of what you recommended and why. When questioned later, you have a clear trail showing ethical choices.

Treat accessibility as a baseline. Check keyboard navigation, heading structure, alt text, and color contrast. Make it part of your quality definition, not an afterthought.

Your approach depends on your environment. If you're agency-side, screen potential tactics before presenting them. If you're in-house, build policies that protect the organization in the long term. If you manage multiple sites, standardize ethical practices across properties.

The framework is flexible because every situation is different. What doesn't change: if you can't defend it publicly, don't do it privately.

Ethical integrity in SEO is often misunderstood as "playing safe." I see it as choosing foundations that don't collapse when the environment gets stricter. It protects clients from tactics that create future emergencies. It protects your reputation from being attached to schemes that eventually get exposed. It protects your work from requiring constant cleanup.

After enough years in this field, you stop being impressed by cleverness that can't be defended. You start respecting the work that stays standing after the next update, and the update after that.

That's what ethical integrity buys you: outcomes you don't have to apologize for later.

But ethics and patience, while necessary, aren't sufficient on their own. You also need to think beyond the immediate task—to anticipate where search is heading and build accordingly. That's where visionary thinking comes in, the habit that ties everything together and keeps your work relevant as the landscape continues to shift.

HABIT 12: VISIONARY THINKING

THE DAY PAGES STOP FEELING LIKE THE UNIT OF WORK

Most SEOs begin by thinking in pages because that's what the tools show you. A URL ranks. A URL drops. A URL has a technical issue. You fix the thing in front of you, then move on to the next. It's a sensible way to learn, and it works for a while.

Then you hit a situation where the "page" is clearly not the problem.

A site can have hundreds of well-written pages and still feel incoherent because nothing connects. Another site can publish less and still win because the information fits together cleanly, builds authority in a concentrated way, and makes it easy for systems to understand what the brand stands for.

Visionary thinking begins when you stop treating SEO as a pile of individual optimizations and start treating it as an information system that either holds together, or it doesn't.

SEEING THE SITE AS A SYSTEM

Once you start looking at a site as a system, you notice different things.

You notice how authority flows—and how easily it gets wasted. You notice that internal linking isn't a tidy "best practice" but a map of how the organization thinks. You notice that taxonomy decisions cast long shadows. You notice that templated elements can either reinforce cohesion or spread confusion at scale.

You also notice how often site growth is treated like a publishing schedule rather than a design problem. Pages get added because someone has a list of keywords, or because content production needs output, or because a team wants to look busy.

A system behaves differently. A system has structure. A system has intent. A system makes it obvious what belongs, what doesn't, and what the next useful thing should be.

WHEN ENTITIES BECOME MORE IMPORTANT THAN PAGES

Another shift tends to occur. You start noticing that search systems don't just evaluate documents—they evaluate the source of the documents.

That's where entity thinking comes into play. Your brand name, your people, your products, your credentials, your consistency across the web, and the way other sources reference you all start to behave like a layer underneath the pages themselves.

This is why two sites can publish similar content and get very different outcomes. One is treated as a credible source; the other is treated as just another page in the pile. You can feel it in how often the brand gets cited, how easily it gets recognized across contexts, and how quickly new content seems to get "understood."

If you've ever watched a respected organization publish something and get referenced immediately, you've seen this effect. It isn't luck. It's accumulated recognition.

THE ECOSYSTEM IS BIGGER THAN SEARCH

The longer you work in SEO, the harder it is to pretend that SEO lives only inside Google's ten blue links.

People discover information in more places now. AI-generated summaries sit above results. Social platforms drive search-like behavior inside their own ecosystems. Communities and forums shape what people trust. Video and audio change how information gets consumed. Direct navigation and brand search matter more when zero-click interfaces squeeze clicks.

At some point, it becomes obvious that your site is only one node in a wider system. Your visibility is influenced by how information about you moves across the web, not just by what your own pages contain.

When you think this way, you stop chasing individual rankings as though they are the whole story. You start paying attention to whether the brand shows up in the places where decisions get made—and whether your content is being used as a source in other people's explanations.

HOW USER BEHAVIOR CHANGES BEFORE ALGORITHMS DO

A lot of "future of search" talk focuses on algorithms, but the shifts that matter often show up first in people.

You can usually see behavior changing before the industry has a name for it. Mobile adoption was visible long before it became a default assumption. "Research on desktop, transact on phone" showed up in analytics before most content was built for that reality. More conversational searching didn't arrive as a press release— it arrived as messy queries and more complex intent.

More recently, you could see the move toward in-place consumption. Featured snippets reduced some clicks. AI Overviews expanded that effect. Zero-click behavior became normal. The outcome isn't that content stopped mattering. The outcome is that the interface started answering earlier, which changes how visibility should be measured and how content should be structured.

Visionary thinking isn't predicting the future like a fortune teller. It's noticing small, consistent changes in behavior and treating them as early signals rather than noise.

WHERE SEARCH SEEMS TO BE HEADING

If you spend enough time watching the ecosystem, a few directions become hard to ignore.

Retrieval and synthesis are taking up more space. Systems increasingly decide what to pull forward and summarize, not just what to rank. That changes what "winning" looks like for informational queries. The source that gets cited can be more visible than the source sitting in position three.

Expertise is becoming more legible. It's not enough to say "we are experts." Systems and users look for proof: transparent authorship, verifiable credentials, clear methods, and citations that show you aren't improvising.

Formats are blending. Text, images, video, audio, and interactive elements increasingly behave like a single surface. The sites that handle this well don't treat each format as a separate project. They design information so it remains consistent across modalities, with transcripts, clear structure, and extractable takeaways.

Personalization intensifies while privacy limits tracking. That tension is real. You can feel it in how hard attribution becomes and how important brand recognition becomes when you can't rely on perfect measurement.

Authority is more distributed. Backlinks still matter, but they're no longer the only signal. Mentions, citations, expert contributions, and consistent identity across platforms shape how systems and users evaluate sources.

These directions won't unfold exactly as anyone predicts. The timing is messy. The direction is the useful part.

BRINGING VISION DOWN TO GROUND

Visionary thinking becomes valuable when it changes what you build.

It pushes you toward flexible foundations: clean information architecture, durable content that answers real questions, a coherent entity footprint, and a publishing model that produces fewer weak pages and more assets people can rely on. It makes you cautious about tactics that only work under narrow conditions. It nudges you toward capabilities that remain valuable even when the interface shifts again.

It also changes how you run experiments. You start testing small bets earlier—not because you expect an immediate payoff, but because you want learning before the market forces your hand. That learning becomes a form of insurance. When something becomes mainstream, you're not starting from zero.

WHEN YOUR PREDICTIONS MISS

Anyone who has been in SEO long enough has a few predictions they'd like to revise. Video adoption timelines. Voice search forecasts. Hyperlocal behavior shifts. The pace of interface changes. The industry is full of confident forecasts that didn't pan out as expected.

The useful lesson isn't "never predict." It's to build in a way that doesn't require perfect prediction.

Work done for voice often improved snippet performance. Entity work improved performance across multiple surfaces. A better structure improved retrieval and comprehension without relying on a specific feature rollout. When your strategic moves are anchored to fundamentals, timing matters less because the work stays useful.

BUILDING THIS HABIT

If you want to make visionary thinking stick, here's what tends to work:

Watch adjacent spaces. Pay attention to technological developments, interface design, and changes in user behavior in adjacent fields. AI developments, voice interfaces, and visual search—these influence how people will search next.

Ask strategic questions regularly. What's changing in how people consume information? Which quality signals keep getting reinforced? What are forward-looking competitors building? Keep these questions running in the background.

Build for flexibility. Invest in clean information architecture, clear entity signals, and content that works across formats. These foundations adapt better than tactical optimizations.

Test early, small, and often. When you see a potential shift, run small experiments before it's mainstream. The learning is more valuable than perfect execution.

Think in systems, not tactics. Don't just fix pages. Design how information flows, how authority accumulates, how users navigate, and how systems interpret your site.

Your approach depends on your role and industry. If you're agency-side, track patterns across clients to spot early trends. If you're in-house, invest in foundational improvements that survive interface changes. If you manage multiple sites, test new approaches on lower-risk properties first.

The framework is loose because the future is uncertain. What doesn't change: build for durability, test new approaches early, and keep your work oriented toward where discovery is actually going.

Visionary thinking is where the other habits start to feel like a coherent practice rather than a collection of tactics.

It gives patience a purpose because you're building assets that mature over time. It makes ethics feel practical because you're investing in foundations you want to keep. It changes collaboration because you're designing systems that require multiple teams to work together cleanly. It even changes how you approach technical work, because you stop treating fixes as isolated tickets and start treating them as part of a durable information architecture.

In SEO, the future rarely arrives as a single event. It arrives as a series of small shifts that gradually become normal. Visionary thinking is the habit of noticing those shifts early, building in ways that stay useful, and keeping your work oriented toward where discovery is actually going.

The twelve habits you've explored aren't a checklist to complete. They're a foundation to operate from. What comes next depends on how you apply them when the work gets hard, the answers aren't clear, and the pressure is on. That's where habits reveal themselves—and where your career is ultimately defined.

CONCLUSION

THE HABITS THAT OUTLAST EVERYTHING ELSE

SEO has undergone several transformations over the past two decades. Entire categories of tactics have faded away. Platforms that once felt indispensable are now footnotes. Algorithm updates have reshaped how visibility works—sometimes subtly, sometimes abruptly. Each wave has arrived with claims that everything has changed.

What actually changed everything was learning to separate what expires from what compounds.

The twelve habits in this book reflect patterns observed across practitioners who endure—people who remain effective even as tools, platforms, and interfaces evolve. These are not personality traits or innate talents. They are learned behaviors that become instinctive through repeated use. They transfer across industries because they are rooted in how complex systems are understood, navigated, and improved over time.

Taken together, these habits form a way of working that is resilient to volatility. They reinforce one another. They create consistency where others rely on bursts of effort. They allow practitioners to operate calmly in environments that reward overreaction.

WHY THESE HABITS MATTER MORE NOW

The environment in which SEO operates has become more demanding, not less.

AI-mediated discovery has altered how information is surfaced, summarized, and cited. **Traditional ranking** remains important, but it now **coexists with extraction**, synthesis, and attribution behaviors that operate differently—especially in a zero-click landscape where visibility often matters more than traffic.

Entity understanding has raised the bar for credibility. Search systems have become more selective about which sources they treat as authoritative. Content that does not add genuinely new or useful information is increasingly ignored, regardless of how well it is optimized.

User expectations continue to rise. People expect definition, speed, accessibility, and accuracy across devices and contexts. Technical excellence and experience design are no longer differentiators; they are baseline requirements.

Privacy regulations and platform changes have made measurement noisier and less complete. Interpreting data now requires judgment, not just dashboards.

At the same time, the volume of content has grown to a point where differentiation depends on substance rather than execution alone.

In this environment, habits provide stability. Tactics respond to change. Habits absorb it.

WHAT REMAINS UNDER YOUR CONTROL

Search systems will continue to evolve. Interfaces will shift. Competitors will make unexpected moves. New technologies will alter how discovery works. Budgets and priorities will fluctuate.

None of that is controllable.

What remains controllable is how you operate within that uncertainty.

How consistently do you learn? How carefully do you observe before acting? How precisely do you execute technical work? How clearly do you understand user needs? How deliberately do you build authority? How effectively do you work with others? How disciplined your processes remain under pressure. How ethically do you conduct your work? How far ahead are you willing to think?

These internal disciplines matter more than any individual tactic. Experience repeatedly shows that practitioners with strong habits outlast those who rely solely on brilliance.

THE PROFESSIONAL IDENTITY THESE HABITS CREATE

When these habits become part of how you work, something changes.

You stop reacting emotionally to volatility because you recognize familiar patterns. You diagnose problems faster because you've seen their shapes before. You communicate more clearly because you understand how different disciplines think. You make decisions with confidence even when information is incomplete. You earn trust because your recommendations are grounded and defensible. You notice opportunities earlier because you think in longer horizons.

This is professional maturity in SEO. It has little to do with knowing every technical detail or anticipating every algorithm shift. It comes from repeated exposure, reflection, and correction.

It looks calm from the outside because it is built on preparation rather than certainty.

THE PATH FORWARD

Reaching the end of this book does not complete the work. It lays out what the work actually is.

These habits do not develop solely through intention. They emerge through use. They form slowly, often invisibly, as decisions are made under real constraints and real consequences.

You do not need to adopt all twelve at once. Most practitioners don't. Habits tend to develop unevenly, shaped by the problems you face most often. Over time, gaps become apparent, and attention shifts naturally.

What matters is consistency. Repetition. Reflection.

As months pass, behaviors that once required effort begin to feel automatic. Judgments that once felt uncertain become easier to make. Situations that once caused anxiety become familiar.

Years later, those habits define how you work. Others begin to rely on your steadiness during change—not because you predict the future, but because you navigate it well.

THE COMPOUNDING EFFECT

This book began with a simple claim: long-term SEO excellence is defined more by professional habits than by tools or tactics.

The practitioners who tend to share the same traits keep learning, while others stall. They ground decisions in evidence rather than speculation. They execute carefully. They focus on users. They build authority patiently. They adapt without panic. They work well with others. They rely on systems rather than memory. They choose integrity over shortcuts. They think beyond the immediate task.

Those habits create an advantage that is difficult to replicate quickly. Not because the work is secret, but because the discipline required to sustain it is rare.

You now have a clear picture of what those habits look like in practice.

What happens next depends on whether they become part of how you work when pressure is high, information is incomplete, and outcomes are uncertain. That is where habits reveal themselves.

12 Habits of Successful SEOs

The twelve habits are not a checklist to complete. They are a foundation to operate from.

Build on it.

APPENDIX 1: INDUSTRY VOICES

This appendix brings together reflections from SEO professionals who generously shared their experience and observations. Their contributions add depth to the habits discussed in this book and highlight the diversity of practice within the SEO community. To ensure fairness and transparency, entries appear in alphabetical order by surname. I am grateful for their willingness to lend their voices to this project.

EDWARD BATE

SEO Consultant, Sydney, Australia

Habit 8: Collaboration Without Friction

"It's crucial to learn the language of your client and adapt to it - Trello or JIRA, how they structure requests and what level of detail to provide, who controls triage and prioritization of tasks, what higher business priorities do they ladder up to and help achieve, and always be communicating upward in the business around progress on the work you and the client are achieving for the website"

ELIE BERREBY

Head of SEO & AI Search at Adorama, Cyprus

Habit 1: Continuous Learning

"Continuous learning goes hand in hand with adaptability to change. The Search industry has always evolved, but never this fast. It is becoming increasingly complex, which is why I find the area interesting.

I often feel I'm behind, even though I'm reading hours a day, writing more than ever before, and testing many advanced strategies. Continuous learning has a cost because it is time-consuming, but there's also an ego cost because the more you learn, the less you feel you know.

That's what happens when you are constantly discovering new concepts and even disciplines. But learning is beautiful!

Some people get a degree and stop learning. That's not an option when working in the search industry.

When we think we know, we stop learning.

I want to be like a little child and ask the simplest and yet profound questions.

To become a visionary thinker, you have to anticipate, test, and connect the dots. But you cannot think like everyone else. And let's face it, most people are consumers, not creators. There aren't many visionary thinkers on earth. This is true of every discipline.

I recently made incredible discoveries regarding knowledge graphs and AI retrieval pipelines. One is an original discovery, never published anywhere. I shared it with about 4 people worldwide. I don't think I'll ever publish it, but the amount of work required to discover this was mind-blowing.

I understand that working day and night isn't for everyone, but that's why real creators and thinkers are valued: most people cannot do it. And the few who could might not want to pay the price.

But there's something everyone should do, especially when the statements come from people with vested interests: be skeptical.

You learn continuously not by reading but by doing. Be skeptical of a spokesperson paid to disseminate a message. Many statements are helpful and true. Some aren't. That's why you have to learn by doing."

MICHAEL BONFILS

CEO and Founder, DIG (Digital International Group)

Habit 4: Content With A Purpose

"Meaningful content to help users is a gift from the brand to the user. It was never meant to be built as a way to game SERPs, from the beginning of search engines, all of them by the way, not just Google, were to reward the best content and most meaningful content that is highly relatable to the user and their intent. If that content happens to be picked up by other authoritative content resources, that's "Cherry

on the Top" and a worthwhile signal. I have told clients for decades, stop gaming, stop gaming, stop gaming. Just be authentic and act as if you were writing a love letter to someone you care about. Search engines and algorithms will eventually see your value. Don't focus on them, just that user. Your job is not to be a search engine."

JONATHAN BOSHOFF

SEO consultant, Canada.

Habit 2: Data-Driven Decision-Making

"Data is the only way to cut through the noise. SEOs who can navigate through analytics, Search Console, and tracking tools provide endless value to leadership teams. Not because they can make cool reports and dashboards, but because they can turn data into insights and take action on them. "Let's update this page because Google likes freshness" turns into "let's optimize this page for these specific queries because their CTR has dropped in the last three months." With data, SEO stops being a guessing game and a battle of trust. It becomes a system of predictable and scalable growth."

JEAN-CHRISTOPHE CHOUINARD

Sr. SEO Strategist at Tripadvisor, blog at jcchouinard.com

Habits 1, 2, and 12

"My working philosophy has always been to try to foresee what people will be asking, dedicate time in my week to learn about those things, and convert these learnings into

experiments and MVP products so that I can see firsthand how actionable the learnings are, and make sure I can answer questions when they come. The question "How well do we rank in AI search?" was the easiest one to predict. When there is lots of chatter, big business impact, and lots of uncertainty, that is when you have to be forward in reading everything, seeing what competition is doing, building tracking systems, and running experiments, so that when people inevitably start asking about it you can instantly give answers and recommendations based on data-driven results. Learn as much as you can and run experiments before giving recommendations."

BRODIE CLARK

Independent SEO Consultant, Australia

Habits 1, 5 & 7

"Continuous learning is likely the biggest driver for me in staying motivated as a consultant and business owner. This goes for attracting the best clients to work with, and also ensuring that the work remains interesting and engaging by remaining in touch and involved with the industry at large. This past year, my continuous learning has been best applied through starting a new business within the software space, which has required the development of many new skills."

JACK CLARK

SEO and AI Automation Consultant, Australia

Habit 7: Adaptability to Change

"Change is constant in this space, now more than ever. I see the best operators lean into it with a smile and embrace every shift as a new opportunity to learn, grow, and innovate. SEO rewards people who genuinely enjoy being relentless problem solvers, and that mindset is what keeps you steady in a field where you have to adapt to new problems every single day"

GIANLUCA FIORELLI

SEO and AI Search Consultant at www.iloveseo.net

Habit 1: Continuous Learning

"I made mine the classic quote from Socrates: 'I know that I know nothing.' This is the only correct mindset for continuously learning, and not fearing new things (not only in Search, but also in life, I would say). Obviously, this doesn't mean we should fall into a sort of impostor syndrome; on the contrary, to be able to recognize that what we have learned is not always written on marble, and that it can change and mutate. And this leads to continuous experimenting and testing."

DUANE FORRESTER

AI and Search Strategist, California.

Habit 1: Continuous Learning

"Search now evolves at the speed of AI, not the speed of blue links. The SEOs who succeed build a learning rhythm that

matches that pace, studying retrieval patterns, model behavior, and the signals machines increasingly favor."

Habit 2: Data-Driven Decision-Making

"Modern SEO becomes far more effective the moment you anchor decisions in evidence. When your work is guided by real signals (how content is discovered, retrieved, and engaged with), your strategy becomes clearer, more predictable, and easier to scale."

Habit 4: Content With Purpose

"Content performs best when it helps someone accomplish something. In an AI-driven world, clarity and structure matter as much as insight because both people and machines rely on them to understand meaning and deliver relevance."

Habit 9: Process Discipline

"SEO scales when it runs on systems, not heroics. Process discipline turns expertise into repeatable outcomes, protecting teams from volatility and ensuring improvements compound over time."

Habit 12: Visionary Thinking

"Successful SEOs think in ecosystems, not fragments. Visibility now depends on how your content flows through retrieval models, entity structures, and knowledge systems, not just where it sits on a page. Vision comes from seeing the whole system the machine sees."

SAIJO GEORGE

SEO/GEO Consultant Melbourne.

Habit 1: Continuous Learning

"Run something on the side. Honestly, this is where the real learning happens. When it's your site, your money, your risk - you learn faster. You try things you'd never get approval for on a client project. You understand the pressure of making decisions that actually matter. It's like the difference between reading about swimming and jumping in the pool."

Habit 5: Relentless User Focus

"Talk to the business owners (and actually listen.) Not just a quick chat - really understand what they're dealing with day-to-day. The people on the ground know things that never make it into briefing documents. They know which products customers actually ask about, which queries drive sales, and which problems keep coming up. That context changes everything about how you approach SEO. You stop optimizing for rankings and start optimizing for outcomes that matter."

GAGAN GHOTRA

SEO Consultant, Melbourne, Australia

Habit 1: Continuous Learning

Search is changing almost every week now! Knowing and making decisions accordingly is really important because one decision can set the client 10x ahead of the competition, like if Google introduces a search feature, already thinking of ways to optimize for it.

Habit 2: Data-Driven Decision-Making

Understanding data, extracting insights from it, and turning those insights into actionable items to implement on the client's site is really important for moving the needle on SEO performance and, therefore, revenue. Nowadays, for most of my SEO workflows, I'm using Claude to analyze data and prepare recommendations (of course, it hallucinates and makes mistakes). However, it's still way better than spending hours and hours analyzing when you could get the recommendations sorted and focus on implementation.

Habit 12: Visionary Thinking

Right now, with AI, everything is changing! Google is deploying different models across its products, and how users interact with Google is changing almost every week. Moreover, for a while, Google has been running specific, limited product features experiments - they call it Google Labs. I've been keeping an eye on it and using the newly introduced products/features to get a sense of where Google Search and Google as a company are heading. I recommend all the SEOs and marketers to also watch out for these new features because, in the future, when these are integrated into Google ecosystems, it's going to change the buyers' funnel and conversion journey from getting introduced to a product to actually buying it.

MIKE GINLEY

Digital Strategy Lead, Chicago, IL

Habit 8: Collaboration Without Friction

"There have been so many changes with tech stacks, algorithms, and ways of working that SEOs probably work with more teams/specialists than any other area in digital.

It is so important to build solid relationships with everyone you work with to ensure work can get done on time. Any breakdowns with teams and ways of working will impact work getting out the door and the eventual results for SEO."

KEITH GOODE

SEO Product Manager, The Permanente Medical Group, Round Rock, TX, USA

(See Appendix 2)

RACHEL HESELTINE

VP of SEO, Paramount Skydance—USA

Habit 7: Adaptability to Change

"The only constant in SEO is change. While sometimes you can kind of predict the direction of the change, that's not always the case. So it's important to keep a clear head, and to have the ability to pivot in the direction of the change, once you've determined what that direction is (remembering that initial observations may have other factors involved, as nothing is ever done in isolation)."

Habit 11: Ethical Integrity

"Working in-house for a large enterprise, you have to practice ethical SEO as much as possible, the last thing you want is for the site to get hit with a penalty, or an algorithm update, and then have to scramble to try to get back to where you were. That said, there may be times when upper management want to push a project that's "up against the line," then your responsibility is to raise those objections, and clearly lay out the potential risks should they continue down that path."

ADAM HUMPHREYS

Founder / SEO at Making 8 Inc

Habit 1: Continuous Learning

"We actively promote and share our findings with the industry daily. Notably, the Search Marketing Mastermind on Facebook has been running for fifteen years. Social media tends to lean toward narcissistic tendencies rather than value-driven content, and so we often find private Slack channels more constructive. We try to avoid confirmation bias, groupthink-type content, and opt for more professional studies from people actively doing the work, patents and peer-reviewed content when making recommendations."

Habit 2: Data-Driven Decision-Making

"A lot of these signals are good, but when it boils down to it, the KPIs of most organizations, while wanting to grow awareness as market leaders, are to continue to grow their

bottom line. This means measuring real metrics like form fills, call tracking, direct sales conversions and any leads that result in direct business growth. Most fly-by-night operations rely on smokescreens of superficial traffic, and we differentiate ourselves by showing complete transparency while delivering measured bottom-line growth."

Habit 3: Technical Precision

"Relationship building with customers is about enhancing the customer site experience in ways that set you apart. This means getting to the point immediately without making them look. Complete intentionality and client feedback are consistently growing."

Habit 4: Content With Purpose

"We create content that reflects genuine needs, search intent, and attention spans. Website content should immediately address concerns and offer the option to convert, as we've found that even on legal sites, 80 percent of visitors don't read far. If it's helpful, shareable, original, and enhances your brand in respect to attention spans, then you're on the right track. Content should reflect real solutions to common problems in a way that your competition hasn't."

Habit 5: Relentless User Focus

"While many SEOs emphasize long-form content, we actually encourage the opposite. As long as you're answering questions in full, it should be no longer than is necessary in respect for people's time and attention. The site experience with dark mode is somewhat controversial at

the moment, suggesting that most sales occur during consistent periods. Still, one has also to factor in that sales aren't on the first interaction, which means that a glaring white screen at night can be brutal on the eyes."

Habit 6: Strategic Link Building

"We don't emphasize link building for the sake of trying to manipulate search engines. We place intentional copywritten pieces into related spaces where customers are that has evergreen presence. We discourage people from placing relevant content on irrelevant sites, as it reflects poorly on the brand if it appears on a spammy website. Internal links remain one of our most focused on targets as this continues to have a profound impact."

Habit 7: Adaptability to Change

"We used to obsess over SEO algorithm updates when they first came out, but now tend to wait a few weeks, since, as is the case most of the time, they're targeting spammers. If you've been doing the right things, most changes probably don't impact you. Worthy of note: interactions carry such heavy weight over time that it's important to keep all core pages current with the latest content."

Habit 8: Collaboration Without Friction

"We white-label for multinational marketing organizations and agencies pretty regularly. What helped us win consistently was complete transparency and dedicating extra time to communication, rather than mindlessly forcing redundant industry content like other consulting agencies. We also showed working solutions, including code, in our technical SEO audits so that developers could

implement our recommendations, whereas most just spout boilerplate crawl data."

Habit 9: Process Discipline

"We've come to appreciate that relationships with customers often trump results. There's a line between communication and taking too much of the customer's time. Feeling out the customer's needs and implementation requirements on a rolling basis is essential to client growth. Some clients are happy to go a quarter without much talk because they were so happy with the reporting automation."

Habit 10: Strategic Patience

"Managing customer expectations is what sets professionals apart from scammer agencies and slick salesmen who guarantee things they can't, like specific Google results or specific financial winnings. We've found that we've turned away from too emotionally driven customers to growth-minded customers looking to long-term growth over having to burn the house down from spammy processes on the regular."

Habit 11: Ethical Integrity

"Too many agencies take very vulnerable, impressionable owners to the cleaners by using spammy content that tanks their business while charging them a considerable fee to do it. We've found a line between explaining what we do and oversimplifying it through analogies, because then the assumption is that it's too easy. Knowing what to do at the right time and place is often all the difference."

Habit 12: Visionary Thinking

"The truth is, when we started, we were thinking more about search engines, and now we're thinking more about the customer than ever. Interactions on proper search engines are weighted so heavily toward site interactions now that Google has stated that, even if they think they got things right, if the client's search shows otherwise, they'll drop or even remove your search results. In other words, your work should be client-focused at all times."

DIXON JONES

CEO of InLinks/Waikay, England.

Habit 1: Continuous Learning

"To facilitate Habit 1 in our organization, we email daily SEO news directly into a shared Microsoft Teams account, to try to keep up with the news. I did my MBA in my 50s, and this year, at 60, I have bought a high-spec gaming PC specifically to learn how to run AI models locally and use them to make my work more fruitful."

Habit 4: Content with Purpose

"Content with purpose means answering the 'Why' behind the search, not just the 'What.' Successful SEOs don't just fill gaps in keyword volume; they fill gaps in meaning. By focusing on the underlying user intent and semantic context, we create content that serves as the definitive answer for an entity, rather than just another page on the pile."

JESS JOYCE

Organic Growth, Inbound Scope, Canada

Habit 7: Adaptability to Change

"If there ever was a time to be adaptable to change, it's now. I've lived by "the only constant is change," as that's apt for the internet and life (and it's kinda cheeky in dev circles, too), and that idiom rings true in 2025 more than it ever has before.

It may be a bit unfamiliar, as SEO was starting to feel a bit predictable with the changes and adjustments, and with the maturity of Google's algorithm.

AI/LLMs have spiced things up substantially, and we're seeing change at a rate that even seasoned SEOs are spinning their heads over. It's going to be an exciting time ahead as the success will come from iteration and change and testing, just like it always has."

NOAH LEARNER

Noah Learner
Funder, The SEO Community, Colorado, USA

Habit 1: Continuous Learning

"My secret to success lies in consistency. I have spent 400-1200 hours per year focused on continuous learning, coupled with meeting with three external folks each week for the past 7 years. In those meetings, I focus on helping the other person as much as I can. I then follow up on the meeting by doing the thing I promised on the call. And I do

that for three people every week. These meetings help me see wider than others. I also have industry colleagues who are ahead of me by 1-3 years on the path that I'm on, whom I get to meet with 4-12 times a year. These meetings allow me to see farther than others and help me get there faster. This approach came from several places. The first was a blog post by Jason Roberts in 2010 on his Blog, Codus Operandi: https://www.codusoperandi.com/posts/increasing-your-luck-surface-area. In this article, Jason wrote, "The amount of serendipity that will occur in your life, your Luck Surface Area, is directly proportional to the degree to which you do something you're passionate about, combined with the total number of people to whom this is effectively communicated. "I learned about helping others by spending time with Hamlet Batista, JR Oakes, and Dan Leibson, who all encouraged me in different ways to give as much as I can to others. I also had many others who put so much effort into lifting me as I made my way, including Nico Brooks, Dale McGeorge, Derek Perkins, Robin Lord, John Murch, and David Sottimano."

MIKA LEPISTO

Growth Marketing - Hawaii, USA

Habit 5: Relentless User Focus

"SEO isn't separate from customer experience; it's often a mirror of it. Strong search performance usually signals a business that reduces friction, respects user intent, and delivers quality outcomes. Weak SEO may reveal deeper experience problems."

NITIN MANCHANDA

Founder and Chief SEO Consultant at Botpresso, Berlin, Germany

Habit 1: Continuous Learning

"The moment you stop learning in SEO is the moment you fall behind. I treat continuous learning as a nonnegotiable habit, and pair it with an ethical, transparent approach that builds durable trust with users and search engines alike."

CASEY MARKEE

Founder, Media Wyse, United States

Habit 3: Technical Precision

"Technical precision determines whether content is even eligible to perform in modern search. Crawlability, internal linking, rendering, structured data, and performance directly affect how both search engines and AI retrieval systems interpret pages. In an AI-driven answer layer, small technical gaps can completely suppress visibility. Eliminating preventable technical friction through site auditing creates stability and protects long-term growth."

Habit 4: Content With Purpose

"Successful content is written to help users complete a task, not to satisfy keyword formulas. Purpose-driven SEO focuses on clarity, structure, and intent so information can be easily understood, summarized, and cited by users, search engines, and LLMs. In the era of AI Overviews and answer layers, content that lacks clarity is unlikely to be

surfaced or referenced. Clarity is the new standard SEOs should strive to achieve when writing content."

Habit 7: Adaptability to Change

"Search volatility is inevitable as algorithms, SERP layouts, and LLMs evolve. Successful SEOs stay calm, slow down, and diagnose before reacting. Most damage done by site owners following Core or Spam updates is self-inflicted through rushed changes and bad assumptions.

Adaptability isn't constant movement; it's a disciplined response based on evidence."

Habit 10: Strategic Patience

"SEO outcomes compound over time, especially in AI-influenced search environments. Strategic patience means understanding which signals need weeks or months to materialize and resisting the urge to 'fix' what isn't broken. Many traffic losses come from misdiagnosis, not algorithms. Site owners and SEOs are more successful when they view outcomes through a long-term growth lens over short-term panic."

MICHAEL MARTINEZ

SEO Theorist, USA

Habit 1: Continuous Learning

"I allocate time every month to research and - when available - watching lectures and technical presentations from search engine employees."

Habit 2: Data-Driven Decision-Making

"I live in the charts, but one of the pitfalls of data-driven decisions is the risk of overlooking or overestimating the significance of anomalies in the data. I see way too many shallow analyses in the SEO blogosphere. It's hard to say whether people are trying to be concise or if they've missed something potentially important."

Habit 3: Technical Precision

"I think the definition may be a bit overoptimistic. We're all human, and we make mistakes. We also all have to deal with time constraints for every project. In an ideal world, you can be technically precise about everything. The universe is constantly working to force us to make hard choices."

Habit 4: Content With Purpose

"Not always the case. Some of the most successful content can be last-minute, whimsical, or just randomly obsessed with minutiae, and suddenly it becomes a major point of interest for visitors."

Habit 5: Relentless User Focus

"Pretty much."

Habit 6: Strategic Link Building

"Agreed."

Habit 7: Adaptability to Change

"'Successful SEOs stay calm' is foundational."

Habit 8: Collaboration Without Friction

"I think this seems a bit hopeful. It takes two to collaborate successfully. If the other party is unavailable for any reason, the collaboration fails. That happens a lot in the corporate world. Everyone is busy. I think resilient collaborators succeed where they can and come back later to try to redress unsuccessful efforts. They probably don't think in terms of "failure" so much as "good timing.""

Habit 9: Process Discipline

"I don't think routine tasks should be completely automated. You forget about key details when you do that."

Habit 10: Strategic Patience

"Agreed."

Habit 11: Ethical Integrity

"Always."

Habit 12: Visionary Thinking

"I agree that we should all be forward-looking. But most people don't seem to have the time for that. It's challenging to keep up and even move ahead."

PETER MEAD

SEO Consultant at SEOWorkshop.com, Melbourne, Australia

Habit 5: Relentless User Focus

"Yes, the whole purpose of what we do as SEOs is to connect the person searching with the business offering. No matter

how things change with AI or reduced website traffic, we are still focused on helping the business do well online."

JAMES NORQUAY

Founder - Prosperity Media & Sydney SEO Conference

Habit 1: Continuous Learning

"To truly stay ahead in the SEO industry, operating your own testing environments is non-negotiable; in my experience, it is the single most effective method for anticipating algorithm shifts. However, technical testing must be paired with active immersion. This means digesting SEO news daily, curating updates for your team via internal channels and newsletters like SEO FOMO, and engaging physically with the community. Whether it is attending global masterminds or organizing local initiatives like the Sydney SEO Conference, you must constantly expose yourself to new ideas to remain competitive."

Habit 2: Data-Driven Decision Making

"In the modern landscape, data science and analytics teams are the backbone of successful Digital PR and SEO, particularly at the enterprise level. We have made significant investments in these dedicated roles because intuition is no longer enough. This strictly empirical approach reinforces the importance of maintaining your own digital assets: you must have a sandbox where you can test, learn, and validate data before applying it to client strategy."

Habit 6: Strategic Link Building

"Digital PR is crucial to any strategic SEO campaign, as it creates a defensible advantage. The true power of Digital PR lies in its exclusivity; Tier 1 media placements are difficult to secure and even harder to replicate, allowing you to build an 'authority moat' around your business. In highly competitive niches, low-barrier tactics like basic guest posts or marketplace links simply do not suffice. To win, you must execute campaigns that competitors cannot easily copy."

DAN PETROVIC

AI SEO, Australia

Habit 7: Adaptability to Change

"The pace at which SEO changes is accelerating, so I don't aim to adapt to change; I embrace it fully and try to learn something new every day. Now is not the time to rest on your laurels but to innovate, discover, and share."

GASTON RIERA

Technical SEO Manager, Australia

Habits 1, 7, and 2:

"SEO is always evolving, either as a function or as a traffic channel. What has always worked for me are habits of continuous learning, strong adaptability to change, and a commitment to being data-informed. No decisions should

be made just on hunches for today's technical SEO landscape."

PETER ROTA

Senior Technical SEO Manager at Hub International / SEO Freelancer, Boston, USA

Habit 11: Ethical Integrity:

"Ethical Integrity is something that I strive for in both the information I share online and the work I do for my clients. Money is great, but if it comes with you burning bridges, stealing money from clients, and your sites tanking later, it's not worth it. Once you lose your reputation as an SEO, it's hard to come back from that because everything we do is public."

AL SEFATI

Clarity Digital, LLC, Irvine, California.

Habit 1: Continuous Learning

"I have always tried to stay humble in the field, as it is always changing and evolving. The algorithms change, tech changes, demand and trends change, so staying humble has always kept me on my toes to learn, adapt, and evolve to stay current and relevant (and employed)."

RASMUS SØRENSEN

Global eCom SEO Director, Hunter Douglas, Denmark

Habit 10: Strategic Patience

"SEO - and especially for new sites - can take a long time to produce results, even longer if you are in a competitive industry. It takes patience and stakeholder management to be successful in large-scale and enterprise SEO. If you can develop a strong, lasting strategy and have the developers, content team, and digital PR team on board, success will eventually come. Measure, test, and deploy and execute over time."

MARTY WEINTRAUB

Founder, AIMCLEAR®, Minnesota, USA

Habit 9: Process Discipline

"Organic discoverability generates endless possible tasks, but resources are finite. Successful practitioners distinguish between activity and impact. They identify high-impact work, technical fixes that unlock revenue, structural changes that improve efficiency, and ruthlessly cut everything else.

This means saying no to pointless expansions with minimal revenue potential, declining low-value requests from stakeholders, and abandoning initiatives that feel productive but don't move core metrics.

Prioritization ruthlessness requires discipline: tracking effort-to-impact ratios, killing projects that aren't working, and resisting the urge to optimize everything. It means accepting that some content will remain imperfect, other opportunities will be ignored, and non-productive requests will be declined.

The best practitioners protect their focus, invest time where it compounds, and understand that doing less, but doing it well, outperforms scattered effort across channels from classic SEO to visibility on AI Overview SERPs, answer engines, and other discoverability layers. Strategic prioritization prevents burnout, accelerates progress, saves time, and earns money."

NATALIA WITCZYK

CEO @ Mosquita Digital, Barcelona, Spain

Habit 11: Ethical Integrity:

"SEO Consulting is all about trust. The client chooses you, trusts you, and depends on you. And they are often clueless about pricing fairness, which SEO tactics actually move the needle, and what level of impact to expect from a project. They need to trust you. As AI adoption grows among marketing professionals, only those who are trusted will survive. Human connection will be the consultant's main selling point. Ethics will set professionals apart.

An ethical approach brings much more than satisfaction and fulfillment; outstanding integrity builds client retention and long-term trust that lasts a lifetime. More than once, a marketing manager kept hiring the same trusted vendors anytime they moved roles. Getting burned wasn't an option; they wanted those who'd proven themselves. On top of that, *high ethics generates word of mouth. Endorsements are the most sustainable way of finding new business. Ethical consulting pays off."*

APPENDIX 2: BY KEITH GOODE

My good friend, Keith Goode, gave a detailed, thoughtful response that deserves its exclusive space here.

Keith provides a detailed, habit-by-habit response, offering his expert opinion refined over twenty-five years in the SEO industry.

Habit 1: Continuous Learning.

"Yes, continuous learning is required after twenty-five years in SEO, but the discipline doesn't change daily; ranking systems are refined over time. The shift in SERP layouts and AI is an extension of Google's promise to be an "answer engine." True continuous learning is about understanding industry happenings and being observant of your analytics, not necessarily following patents or experimenting on your own site, as this is often unfeasible in a corporate environment. The most important aspect is maintaining a flexible, scientific mindset, as today's best practices may change completely in the future. A flexible mindset is a better habit than just "continuous learning."

Habit 2: Data-driven Decision-making.

"I agree 100 percent. Data-driven decision-making is essential in any serious business. It involves not just analyzing past performance but also using that data to forecast future efforts. This ties into the LOE-LOI (Level of Effort/Level of Impact) matrix, where you prioritize quick wins (low effort, high impact) and long-term strategic items (high effort, high impact) for executive approval. This

approach is critical for proving SEO's value to executives who may be looking for an excuse to see it as guesswork and defund it."

Habit 3: Technical Precision.

"I question the wording, but agree that technical SEO is foundational for both traditional SEO and new AI optimization. If a bot cannot access your content due to issues like no-index tags, robots.txt disallows, or poor coding, you won't appear in search results. A skilled SEO must be able to work backward to diagnose problems and think forward to engineer a site that avoids common issues related to code, accessibility, and server performance."

Habit 4: Content with a Purpose.

" This is a good habit. While the first customer is the search engine, the ultimate user is the human behind the query. Understanding user intent is crucial for structuring and writing content that motivates them. This requires alignment across multiple disciplines, such as video, storytelling, and paid campaigns. It's also important to recognize that some content's purpose is to answer a question, and AI Overviews may serve this traffic without ever landing on our site. We should be okay with this and focus on capturing traffic that is meaningful for conversion and community building, not just all traffic."

Habit 5: Relentless User Focus.

"We cannot directly associate these user-focused elements with search performance (causality). Metrics like accessibility, readability, and task completion are measured after a user lands on the site. While there's a suspected

correlation between good user interaction and rankings, we don't have a proven one-to-one connection. The focus is not just on acquiring traffic, but on how we treat the user post-click to address their original search intent."

Habit 6: Strategic Link Building.

Keith: I have nothing to add to this habit.

Habit 7: Adaptability to Change.

"This habit overlaps with the first two (continuous learning and technical precision). Adaptability is crucial. The most annoying people in SEO are those who proclaim "SEO is dead" after every change, reflecting a personality uncomfortable with change or hard-coded to outdated practices. Flexibility is vital because when you have it, you can adapt your efforts rather than panic. This is particularly true for those who rely on short-term tricks, like certain link-building tactics, and panic when those stop working, missing the larger point of the discipline."

Habit 8: Collaboration without Friction.

"Yes, this is especially true in a corporate environment. In smaller organizations, an SEO might wear many hats and merely collaborate with themselves. In larger ones, collaboration is vital. A key part of my approach has always been education: teaching developers to write crawlable code, working with designers on effective and AI-friendly layouts, and guiding content teams beyond simple keyword lists to a deeper understanding of user needs. SEOs should also aim for product management roles in the long term, understanding agile or Kanban methodologies to work

effectively within the organization. This is one of the most important soft skills for an SEO."

Habit 9: Process Discipline.

"I agree, but this is more of an organizational responsibility than just an SEO's. Ensuring past failures aren't repeated through systems like Kanban or Agile is the responsibility of the entire organization. While SEOs are part of this, these are requirements of being part of an organization, not unique to the SEO role itself."

Habit 10: Strategic Patience.

"I agree with this habit. It is something younger or newer SEOs won't have right away and must learn over time through experience. Understanding timelines for different situations, like a site migration versus a rehabilitation, comes from doing the work, not just reading about it. I would almost call this habit "strategic patience (with wisdom)" because it's not easily learned."

Habit 11: Ethical Integrity.

"This almost goes without saying, as the industry has been forced into more ethical practices. Black-hat tactics are short-lived before penalties arrive. It's cynical, but we act ethically because the overarching algorithm monitors for bad behavior. When buying backlinks worked and wasn't punished, every SEO was doing it. So, it's less about "ethical integrity" and more about risk tolerance. Risk-averse SEOs act ethically, while risk-tolerant SEOs are seen as unethical or black-hat."

Habit 12: Visionary Thinking.

"I somewhat disagree. Most SEOs react to changes; we can't foresee SERP evolution beyond maybe a few months or a year. The idea of a "visionary" SEO is challenged by the reality of corporate budget, funding, and resource allocation. Executive levels have a very low tolerance for visionary thinking, unlike the "fail fast" startup culture of the late 90s. Today, companies are prioritizing shareholder bonuses over advancing the business. SEOs are therefore forced to react to changes rather than proactively plan. Many want to be visionary but are unable to due to these external business factors."

NOTES

SEO Ethics: "Ethical integrity" in SEO is less about genuine moral conviction and more about pragmatic risk management. It's a forced adaptation to avoid penalties and algorithmic monitoring, rather than an intrinsic commitment to transparency or sustainability. This redefines ethical behavior as a function of risk tolerance rather than as an inherent moral principle.

Ideal SEO Collaboration: Ideal collaboration is a continuous process of education and alignment across departments. It's about SEOs actively teaching developers to create "crawlable code" and working with designers to ensure "engaging design" that also considers how AI consumes content. They also see SEOs guiding content teams beyond mere "keyword lists" to a deeper understanding of "user needs". Ultimately, this collaboration involves SEOs understanding and integrating into "Agile or Kanban structures" and even aspiring to "product management roles" to weave SEO insights into the organizational fabric effectively.

Reframing SEO Habits as Core Competencies for Pragmatic SEOs:

The list of SEO habits could be reframed as "Core Competencies for Pragmatic SEOs" or "Strategic Mindsets for Modern SEO," emphasizing the underlying approach and corporate realities. This would involve:

1. Integrating Nuance and Context: Directly incorporating my (Keith's) interpretations, especially regarding corporate constraints and the "why" behind each habit.
2. Emphasizing Flexibility and Experience: Highlighting the adaptive and wisdom-driven aspects of successful SEO.
3. Reframing Idealistic Terms: Adjusting habits like "Ethical Integrity" and "Visionary Thinking" to reflect a more pragmatic, risk-managed perspective.

For example:

- Instead of "Continuous Learning," consider "Cultivating a Flexible, Scientific Mindset": This captures the need for adaptability and an evidence-based approach, acknowledging that learning involves evolving viewpoints and observing analytics, rather than always experimenting on corporate sites.

- Instead of "Data-Driven Decision-Making," consider "Data-Driven Justification and Forecasting": This highlights the essential role of data in proving SEO's value, securing resources, and predicting outcomes within corporate structures.
- Instead of "Ethical Integrity," consider "Risk-Managed Practice": This reflects the pragmatic view that ethical behavior is often driven by the avoidance of penalties and long-term damage, rather than inherent morality.
- Instead of "Visionary Thinking," consider "Strategic Adaptation within Constraints": This acknowledges that modern SEOs often react to industry shifts and operate within budget and risk-aversion limits, rather than proactively shaping the future.

www.ingramcontent.com/pod-product-compliance
Lightning Source LLC
Chambersburg PA
CBHW051806050726
47598CB00006B/2452